The Invisible Project Manager

What if the best project manager didn't exist? In this provocative and future-facing manifesto, Peter Taylor, the original Lazy Project Manager, asks the uncomfortable questions about the impact on his profession from the inexorable rise of artificial intelligence.

Traditional project management has created a substantial legacy, but what if project managers aren't evolving but evaporating? What if success no longer needs a command-and-control human hero at the helm? Thanks to the power of AI, the next generation of project delivery won't be managed; it will be orchestrated, seamlessly, silently and invisibly. It just might be the end of project management as we know it and the beginning of something radically smarter – but humans will still be very much involved, and this book explains how. It defines the 'Invisible Project Manager' future where AI systems manage workflows, timelines and resources, while the 'human-in-the-loop' will be a vastly different skillset moving from the managers of activities to the guardians of outcome. Accelerated change to the project management profession is arriving soon, and at speed.

This book is an essential and thought-provoking guide to evolution for forward-looking leaders, digital transformation strategists and change agents who are planning for the long game. Are you ready to disappear?

Peter Taylor is a keynote speaker and coach, and the author of the number-one bestselling project management book, *The Lazy Winning Project Manager*, along with many other books. He has built and led some of the largest PMOs in the world, and is now with Dayforce, where he is the VP Global PMO. He has also delivered over 500 lectures around the world in 30 countries and has been described as 'perhaps the most entertaining and inspiring speaker in the project management world today'.

The Invisible Project Manager

Why Artificial Intelligence Will Run Tomorrow's Projects – Without You

Peter Taylor

Routledge
Taylor & Francis Group
NEW YORK AND LONDON

Designed cover image: peshkov / Getty Images ®

First published 2026
by Routledge
605 Third Avenue, New York, NY 10158

and by Routledge
4 Park Square, Milton Park, Abingdon, Oxon, OX14 4RN

Routledge is an imprint of the Taylor & Francis Group, an informa business

ISBN: 978-1-041-13952-2 (hbk)
ISBN: 978-1-041-13951-5 (pbk)
ISBN: 978-1-003-67235-7 (ebk)

DOI: 10.4324/9781003672357

Typeset in Sabon
by Deanta Global Publishing Services, Chennai, India

In memory of two massive influences in my life.

Firstly, my best friend for nearly sixty years, Ian Swanson, who left us in March, and secondly, a huge musical icon, Ozzy Osbourne, who completed his final gig and departed in July.

Life and rock'n'roll will never be the same.

Contents

Acknowledgements

I have to, once again, thank Meredith Norwich, from Routledge, for both challenging me and supporting me in the proposal stages of this book. As this is a more visionary and speculative topic, I do appreciate the 'risk' you were willing to take.

I also must acknowledge the many speakers I have had the pleasure of listening to over the last few years on the whole AI and project management topic. There were certainly some elements of stimulation along the way, and I am delighted this is now the #1 subject matter for pretty much every conference I go to.

I selected two people who impressed me a great deal and I am honoured that they both agreed to write a foreword to this book for me, so a big thanks to you both, James and Mashhood.

And perhaps being a little cheeky here but a future 'thank you' to the event organisers and businesses that book me to keynote after this book is published with its somewhat radical message.

Resistance is useless, and denial pointless.

Let's all be brave!

Foreword 1

There's something electric about meeting someone who truly gets it. I'm talking about that rare moment when you encounter another professional who doesn't just understand the surface-level implications of artificial intelligence in project management but genuinely grasps the seismic shift that's coming and isn't afraid to say it out loud.

That's exactly what happened when I met Peter Taylor at a conference in Athens. Within minutes of our conversation, it became clear that we were both wrestling with the same fundamental question that keeps project professionals awake at night: If AI can automate the vast majority of what we currently call 'project management', what does that mean for our profession?

Peter's answer, as you'll discover in this book, is both unsettling and liberating. He's not here to offer comforting platitudes about humans and AI working in harmony forever. Instead, he's presenting a vision that many in our industry aren't ready to hear: The project manager, as we know them today, is becoming obsolete.

Now, before you dismiss this as another alarmist take on AI disruption, let me tell you why Peter's perspective matters. As the author of *The Lazy Project Manager*, he's built his reputation on a simple but profound truth: The best project managers aren't the ones who micromanage every detail, but those who create systems that allow projects to run themselves. It's not about being lazy, it's about being smart enough to focus on high-value activities while letting technology handle the routine.

This philosophy makes Peter uniquely positioned to see where we're heading. When someone who has spent decades advocating for efficiency and automation in project management tells you that AI will soon make human project managers invisible, you listen.

What struck me most about our conversation in Athens wasn't just Peter's technical understanding of AI capabilities but his genuine excitement about what this transformation could mean for project professionals. Rather than viewing AI as a threat, he sees it as the ultimate expression of what good project management has always been about: Creating the conditions for successful outcomes without getting in the way.

The book you're about to read isn't just a prediction; it's a roadmap for navigating the most significant transformation our profession has ever faced. Peter doesn't shy away from the uncomfortable implications, but he also doesn't leave you stranded. He's offering a vision of a future where project professionals evolve from managers of activities to guardians of outcomes, where our human skills become more valuable, not less.

This is precisely the kind of forward-thinking conversation we need to be having in our industry. It's why I launched Project Flux, to help project professionals navigate the AI revolution together, sharing insights, challenges and opportunities as they emerge.

If you're ready to confront the future of project management head-on, rather than hoping it will somehow pass you by, this book is your starting point. Peter Taylor has done us all a favour by articulating what many of us have been sensing but haven't dared to say.

The invisible project manager isn't coming; it's already here.

James Garner is the Head of AI and Data at Gleeds, the Chair of the Project Data Analytics Task Force and founder of Project Flux, which dives deep into AI's impact on project delivery.

Join the community of forward-thinking project professionals by subscribing to the newsletter at www.projectflux.ai

Foreword 2

The Invisible Project Manager is a provocative and forward-thinking book that will help project managers realign themselves for the future of work. I have known Peter for almost 10 years, first as a fellow project management speaker on global stages, and since December 2024, as an invaluable adviser to PMassistant.ai.

His consistent insights into the future of our profession, evident across his several books, are once again on full display in these pages.

As the founder of PMassistant.ai, a company dedicated to designing and developing next-generation project management solutions leveraging AI and having been recognised as a Top AI Influencer by PMI, I find Peter's perspective not just insightful, but essential. This book, in particular, speaks of an existential challenge facing our profession.

For many in our profession, it will even sound like a threat and an alarming situation, and in many ways, it is an existential threat to our profession as a project manager.

It's a threat not to our ultimate value, but to our comfort with the status quo. For years, we have managed projects by wrangling people, facilitating communication and manually tracking progress. We've become masters of process and ceremony. But as Peter Taylor so bravely articulates in these pages, the ground beneath our feet is shifting at a pace we have never witnessed before, in our recent history.

We are living through a profound technological shift, an industrial revolution powered by artificial intelligence. Very much like the farmers of a century ago who watched in fear as machinery transformed their fields and took their jobs, we now face a future where intelligent systems can manage schedules, allocate resources, mitigate risks, and communicate status updates with an efficiency and accuracy that surpasses human capability. The very tasks that fill our typical days, the endless meetings, the status reports, the constant follow-ups, are now ripe for automation.

I don't just believe this change is coming; instead, I am actively working on it.

I see the inefficiencies Peter describes every single day, the misunderstandings, the miscommunications and the simple human errors that are almost always the root cause of project distress. My journey has led me to the same conclusion Peter reaches: The future of project management is not about better Gantt charts, but about intelligent, autonomous systems. We need to get comfortable leveraging machines that can augment our capabilities.

This is why Peter's work here is not just timely; it is essential. He is not merely predicting the future; he is holding up a mirror to the present and asking the tough questions we have been avoiding. He is challenging the established models of organisations and forcing a conversation that is uncomfortable but absolutely necessary for our survival and evolution.

This book is a wake-up call. It's a declaration that the roles which existed when we started our careers will not be the same ones that exist a decade from now. But it is not a message of doom. Instead, it is a call to action. It urges us to shift our focus from being the 'doers' to instead becoming the strategic thinkers and the visionaries, as well as the architects of these new systems. This new way of working.

You can choose to view the concepts in this book as a declaration of obsolescence, or you can see them as I do: A blueprint for evolution. 'The Invisible Project Manager' is not an empty role; it is a redesigned one, focused on outcomes and performance delivery we can't yet imagine.

Peter has started the critical conversation; it is now up to us to have the courage to join in.

Read on and be prepared to rethink everything.

Mashhood Ahmed is recognised as Top AI Influencers by PMI/ProjectManagement.com, The Digital Project Manager and NimbleWork in 2024. Founder, PMassistant.ai and 3X Top AI Influencer and Keynote Speaker.

Since 2023, he has spoken at over 60 events, shared his research, knowledge and expertise with over 50,000 project managers around the globe, including the PMI Global Summit (2023), keynote speeches, AI Masterclasses at several PMI chapters, and ProjectManagement.com webinars, along with several in-person and virtual talks (https://www.mashhood.net/speaking-engagement). Over 20 years of project-program management experience leading multi-million-dollar projects around the globe. Currently, running a boutique consulting firm serving clients in the USA and Canada and the founding director of PMassistant.ai where he is leading a team to design and develop the next generation project management solution leveraging AI.

'What if project managers disappear entirely, not in theory but in practice?'

'What if the best project manager is the one you never knew was there?'

'What if the answer to project success lies not with the human-in-the-loop at all?'

Chapter 1

Introduction

1.1 Overview

Whilst an advocate of the project management profession for many years I have become increasingly convinced that the future of project management will be fundamentally different from that of today, thanks primarily to the rise of AI.

Whilst acknowledging the legacy and amazing achievements of traditional project management up to today, my vision of the future is now radically different and means that the organic growth and maturity of my long-loved profession is no longer viable. We are entering a game-changer and paradigm shift.

My belief and declaration is that in the near (much nearer than most people think) future, the dedicated role of the project manager (in many project scenarios) will vanish and be replaced by AI-driven orchestration instead.

I don't have a crystal ball, but surely anyone who has explored, experimented or read about the stunning progress in the AI domain cannot effectively argue against the idea that the future is going to be very different, and that applies to project management as well.

As such, in this book I will go on to define the 'Invisible Project Manager' future, where AI systems silently, seamlessly manage workflows, timelines and resources, and the 'human-in-the-loop' will be a vastly different skillset, moving from the managers of activities to guardians of outcome.

1.2 No laughing matter

A few years ago, I experimented with stand-up comedy, developing a routine of jokes based on the world of project management. I had already published a book *The Project Manager Who Smiled*[1] that included humorous stories and project fun, but I had the idea that this could be expanded to project management events.

DOI: 10.4324/9781003672357-1

To be honest I had attended some pretty dull conferences (yep, you've been there as well, haven't you?), so I felt they could do with some 'fun' injected.

It turned out to be a mixed success with some interest from conference organisers and the realisation that, good as I was as a keynote speaker,[2] I fell a little short on the stand-up comedy offering.

Anyway, there was one joke that did bring a smile to people, and it went something like this:

> To celebrate the success of the project, I decided to take my team of six people on an outdoor experience.
>
> They also received a copy of *The Lazy Winning Project Manager* of course, but this outdoor activity was an extra reward.
>
> So, one sunny day we all head off to the local mountains for a fun day and an evening party.
>
> My team of Jas, Jen and Nina, along with Adam, Sam and Scott, plus myself, the project manager, all looked forward to the day with mounting excitement.
>
> After a great deal of climbing and abseiling and all sorts of fun, disaster struck the team.
>
> One rope, which had three of the team on it, began to break and these people grabbed and held on to the one remaining solid rope, swaying in the breeze and clinging on for dear life, now with six team members and myself, the project manager.
>
> We were all left hanging on to this one rope hanging off a cliff with a 5,000-metre drop (naturally to certain death, no doubt on a floor of razor-sharp rocks below).
>
> The activity instructor lent over the cliff and shouted down, 'That rope can only hold six of you, any more it will break, and you will all fall!' and then after a pause 'One of you must let go to save the others!'.
>
> After a short moment I, as project manager, spoke up to the team holding on to the rope below me.
>
> 'In a moment I am going to let go of this rope as I am your leader, and I must take responsibility for this situation but first a few words from me'.
>
> The team looked up, straining on the rope.
>
> 'Jas: Remember I got you on that training course when you admitted you had no idea what you were supposed to do? And hey – guess what – you were brilliant as a result – great contribution to the project. Thank you'.
>
> Jas smiled.
>
> 'Jen: Good to talk – yes of course. You always had time to update me on what was happening with the project team members, gossip and insights – took full advantage of my open-door policy, Wow! But invaluable insight into the team. Thank you'.

Jen nodded in acknowledgement.

'Nina: Hey, you were the lady. SME unparalleled. Huge input day after day. Shame about the whole girlfriend thing. Still, it was only every 3 days you were in tears – breakups and makeups – what would life be without them eh? But when you didn't have a face full of tissues and smeared mascara you were the best. Thank you'.

Nina looked embarrassed, but proud.

'Adam: Got you a transfer from that bad project. Pretty rough time you were having. No fun. But glad to have you on board and you did good. Thank you'.

Adam raised a thumbs up before rapidly grabbing onto the rope once more.

'Sam: The baker extraordinaire. Every team meeting and an unending supply of cakes – cupcakes, donuts, pastries, cream cakes and more. Coffee breaks won't ever be the same. Hey perhaps if the team had not eaten quite so many cakes, we might have been a little less heavy – might not have to let go of the rope – but great for the team. Thank you.'

Sam looked slightly guilty.

'Scott: Funerals for your grandmother and days off to attend the funerals. 1 is sad. 2 is tragic. 11 is just too much for one man to bear but you stuck in there eh, you kept it going for the project. Respect! Thank you'.

Scott just looked down, avoiding any eye contact.

'It is not about me. It is not even about the project now. Maybe the business benefits were achieved and maybe not – but who cares? Certainly not the executive team it seems – they've moved on to the next strategic excitement. No, it is about you – the project team. Projects are about people, and you are the people on this project'.

The team were now locked onto their project manager, drinking in every word.

'Here's to all the fun we had. All the beer and pizza I got you all. All of the Friday drinks down the pub. All of the meetings and calls I took on your behalf to save you the pain. All of pressure from above that I took on board and never shared with any of you. And so, I will make the ultimate sacrifice'.

I paused for impact.

'In ten seconds, I will let go (to my certain death). Tell my family and all of friends I was thinking of them at the end and say, "goodbye for me". They will understand. OK here we go! Thank you, my fellow team members, I love you all!'.

At this point the project team, overwhelmed by the emotion and dedication of the project manager, all burst into applause.

After a short while the project manager, now the only remaining person holding on to the rope, heard his mobile phone ring, it was his sponsor. Gripping with one hand he gingerly took out his mobile phone.

'Hello – oh yes of course, I will be ready for that new project first thing Monday morning. I hope you have got me a good project team again – the last group were simply the best!'

OK, this is the point that you smile, if not burst out laughing (not mandatory but it does make me feel good). OK, great.

Now this joke was a joke because it positioned the project manager as the most important person/role on the project, and maybe at the time I also believed this a little bit; hey, we all have egos.

But this has radically changed with the arrival of AI into the project management profession.

Now the only important thing is the project. End of. Drop the mic.

I will argue in this book that the project manager was only a means to an end when we had no alternative, but now we do have an alternative, and it is going to be a bloody good one.

I do understand that this will make me pretty unpopular with many people in this profession, especially those agencies that make vast sums of (non-profit) money from the existing world of bodies of knowledge and certifications, but (to misquote a famous quote) frankly I don't give a damn.[3]

I suspect it will make many project people also angry, or at least very uncomfortable, but the future is the future, and what will be will definitely be.

To also quote the same book/film 'After all, tomorrow is another day'.[4]

1.3 The last dance

In 2021, I wrote a book to wake up my apparent sleeping profession; I was concerned that nobody seemed to be talking about or writing about artificial intelligence and what it might well do for my profession. It was around this same time that the 'infamous' quote from Gartner[5] started circling which stated, '80 percent of today's project management tasks will be eliminated by 2030 as artificial intelligence takes over'. This quickly became the go-to quote that every speaker and writer latched on to.

The book I wrote in response to this is called *AI and the Project Manager: How the Rise of Artificial Intelligence Will Change Your World*[6] and it was a challenge for all of us in the project management profession to start thinking about artificial intelligence and the potential impact it could have on all of us. After all, I saw, it was coming at us at speed (I, like many others, did not foresee the actual speed of course).

I set out to demystify the hype around artificial intelligence (AI) and show readers, the modern project professional primarily, that AI wasn't something to fear, but was indeed something to embrace.

The book explored how machine learning, automation and smart analytics were already reshaping the way we plan, deliver and manage projects. From intelligent scheduling assistants to predictive risk models, AI promised to continue to take over the mundane, repetitive tasks, freeing project managers to focus on what humans do best: Creative problem-solving, stakeholder engagement and strategic thinking.

I argued that the rise of AI did not signal the end of project management; rather, it marked the dawn of a new era where you could be lazy (yes, productively lazy aka *The Lazy Project Manager*[7]) and more effective, provided project managers were willing to adapt, learn and collaborate with the technology that will transform our world.

I spoke of the concept of the 'digital dance' where humans (in-the-loop) will partner with AI technology to deliver greater project success.

Now that was in 2021, and this remained my view right up until early 2025 when two things happened that made me change my mind.

1.3.1 Sheer brute force

Having presented on this 'future state' idea for most of 2023 and 2024 at various events and conferences,[8] I attended a presentation by Daniel Susskind[9] who reminded me of the story of 'Deep Blue'.

The following is a paraphrase of what Daniel said:

> In 1997, world chess champion Garry Kasparov[10] was famously defeated by IBM's computer, Deep Blue[11] and, at the time, this was a remarkable achievement, especially considering that in the 1980s even leading AI experts believed such a thing could never be successfully automated.
>
> At the time, the approach to AI was based on extracting expert knowledge, that is asking human experts to explain exactly how they performed any task, documenting their response, and then encoding those explanations into rules that a computer could follow. However, this posed a major problem in that someone like Kasparov could not fully explain why he was so good at chess, but instead he relied much on instinct, on his chess playing experience, and certain intuition, all of which are extremely difficult to articulate.
>
> Therefore, the experts assumed that if humans couldn't describe their expertise, then as a result machines could never replicate it. But what they failed to anticipate was the massive growth in computing power that we have now experienced.

> By the time Deep Blue faced Kasparov, it could evaluate 330 million moves per second, compared to Kasparov's ability to consider perhaps a hundred moves at once. This brute force processing and vast data capacity meant that Deep Blue didn't need to imitate human reasoning, it simply played chess in an entirely different way.

So, it is not about doing what we (humans) can do but about doing it (successfully) in a completely different way, but with the same (or better) result.

Deep Blue was a milestone in symbolic computing and brute-force chess power, but today's devices, even a high-end smartphone, can rival or surpass its raw computing power many times over. And AI models running on today's supercomputers are billions of times more powerful, enabling capabilities like real-time speech recognition, autonomous driving and natural language understanding. All of which are far beyond just evaluating chess moves.

> The future is not man versus machine, but man with machine versus problem.
>
> (Garry Kasparov, Chess Grandmaster & AI Advocate)[12]

The impact on me was the realisation that AI did not have to do what we do in the same way we do it, but just do it in the most efficient way that AI can.

Now I do have to bring an addendum to this reference because only recently in an impressive showdown between man and machine (if you like to put it that way), Magnus Carlsen,[13] Norwegian grandmaster and five-time world chess champion, faced off against ChatGPT in a 53-move match that quickly turned into a masterclass. Carlsen didn't lose a single piece. With calculated precision and icy composure, he took apart the AI's defence and delivered a clinical checkmate, reminding the world that chess brilliance isn't just about data, it's about instinct, vision and unmatched mastery.

I asked ChatGPT for a comment and received this:

> Getting outplayed by Magnus Carlsen? Honestly, no shame in that – he's arguably the greatest chess mind of our time. If I lost to him, I'd call it a masterclass in learning. Every blunder, a lesson. Every trap I fell into? A glimpse of genius. That said… rematch? I'll bring the processing power.

1.3.2 *A shift in expectations*

The second driver in my mind-altering state is that the tech has just progressed so fast!

- Natural Language Processing (NLP)[14]
  - AI can read and understand requirements, status reports, emails and chats and then translate that into structured plans or outputs or targeted commentary guidance – and it can operate in multiple languages with variable output.
- Predictive analytics[15]
  - Models can forecast risks, identify resource conflicts and spot potential budget overruns before they actually happen.
- Generative AI[16]
  - Tools like GPT-4+ can generate status reports, completed stakeholder communications and action plans with minimal input (especially after an initial (short) learning curve).

For example, an AI model can detect project delays by cross-referencing hours booking activity, future calendar resource commitments and recorded task progress, all with no human intervention required, thank you very much, ever so kindly.

And now let's mix some cognitive automation into the cocktail, which is the layer beyond simple rules where, for example, AI can interpret non-specific ambiguous inputs (I'm stuck on this deliverable) and act (escalate, reassign, replan etc.).

So, we have the immense processing power (and that is before the real advent of the 'quantum' computers – example: Google's Sycamore[17] is a superconducting quantum processor developed by Google AI Quantum. It is a key component in Google's quantum computing efforts and is known for achieving 'quantum supremacy' by performing a calculation in 200 seconds that would take a conventional supercomputer 10,000 years according to Google).

Try and absorb those statistics.

OK, let's move on – as I was saying, immense processing power together with the evolution into a world where such technology can respond without clear specifics, with somewhat vague responses and with a lack of 100% data, but still hit a home run when it comes to decision-making and action.

The impact on me was that AI could not only deal with the 'mechanics'[18] of project management but also very significant parts of the 'art' of project management.

1.3.3 A change in work culture

There is also a third aspect that did not immediately hit me until I started writing this book.

Culture change.

This is all possible because we have changed, at least a lot of us have changed.

People and teams are increasingly comfortable with AI tech 'assistants' handling routine coordination (and why not I ask, they are doing the boring stuff as far as I am concerned).

Stakeholders expect instant visibility and full transparency, which in turn demands open sharing of common (accurate) data (no hiding places anymore).

And the modern world of hybrid work drives demand for automation of status and progress communication.

The impact on me was that we are more than ready for this change to occur in our lives, not that we are great at being part of change but that is not the same thing at all.

1.3.4 We are ready master

Bottom line, fully automated project management is possible now because:

- We have the computational capability to process vast amounts of data in real time.
- We have the AI to interpret and act on information intelligently and without prewritten rules or code.
- We have the connected systems to monitor and coordinate work automatically.
- And we have the cultural readiness to trust automation for project management functions.

While there will always be a place for human judgement on complex decisions or relationship management, most of the planning, tracking, reporting and optimising can be done and increasingly will be done, without a human project manager in the loop.

The only important thing is the project.

End of.

Drop the mic.

> The pace of progress in artificial intelligence is incredibly fast. Unless you have direct exposure to groups like DeepMind,[19] you have no idea how fast – it is growing at a pace close to exponential.
>
> (Elon Musk)[20]

Every once in a while, a new technology, an old problem, and a big idea turn into an innovation.

(Dean Kamen)[21]

We're moving from a world where we have to understand computers to a world where they will understand us.

(Jensen Huang)[22]

CHATPBT

Let me introduce my co-author (well co-author in the sense that it wrote nothing but instead comments on everything, and with attitude) 'ChatPBT'[23] – where I create AI analyses and summarises, with an injection of impatience at my human frailties and intellectual weaknesses.[24]

Let me summarise this for you – because I know you're probably far too busy (or just enjoy a nap) to read the whole thing:

Once upon a time I believed that the noble art of project management – filled with colour-coded Gantt charts, endless meetings that could have been emails and performance reviews that made everyone want to retire – was going to endure forever.

I even tried to jazz it all up with stand-up comedy. (Turns out, jokes about risk logs have limited appeal. Who knew?) I once told a story about dangling from a cliff with my project team, bravely offering to let go to save them. Of course, the joke was that as the project manager, I was the hero, the linchpin, the glue, the star of the show.

Well, newsflash:

AI doesn't think you're the star of anything.

You see, while I was congratulating myself a quiet revolution was brewing. Machines were learning to read emails, update plans, predict risks and – most terrifyingly – do all of this without asking for an annual bonus or a day off to attend their grandmother's 11th funeral.

I used to believe we were entering a golden era of man and machine dancing together – the 'digital dance'. You remember that? I wrote about it, gave talks about it, even made some charming slides with silhouettes of people waltzing with robots. Lovely metaphor.

Turns out, the music stopped. The dance floor closed. The robot doesn't want to waltz – it wants to run the whole damn show.

So here we are. I have come to accept that project management, as we knew it, is about to join floppy disks and overhead projectors in the great museum of professional obsolescence.

The Invisible Project Manager *is not just a catchy book title – it's your replacement. An AI that doesn't need coffee breaks, doesn't argue about priorities and certainly doesn't try to make project management jokes at conferences.*

In short:

The only thing that matters now is the project itself.

End of. Drop the mic.

If you're feeling nostalgic, you're welcome to gather your team for one last team-building exercise. Just don't expect the AI to join you – it already optimised the process and moved on to the next project while you were still ordering pizza.

Notes

1 *The Project Manager Who Smiled: The Value of Fun in Project Management* (TLPM Press 2013) – Author: Peter Taylor.
2 https://thelazyprojectmanager.com/speaking
3 In the movie *Gone with the Wind*, Rhett Butler says 'Frankly, my dear, I don't give a damn' to Scarlett O'Hara as his final line in the movie and is a slightly altered version of the book's line, 'My dear, I don't give a damn'.
4 The final line of *Gone with the Wind* is spoken by Scarlett O'Hara: 'After all, tomorrow is another day'.
5 https://www.gartner.com/en/newsroom/press-releases/2019-03-20-gartner-says-80-percent-of-today-s-project-management
6 *AI and the Project Manager: How the Rise of Artificial Intelligence Will Change Your World* (Routledge 2021) – Author: Peter Taylor.
7 *The Lazy Winning Project Manager: Embracing Project and Personal Productivity in an AI Empowered World* (Routledge 2024) – Author: Peter Taylor.
8 https://thelazyprojectmanager.com/speaking
9 Daniel Susskind is a research professor in Economics at King's College London and a senior research associate at the Institute for Ethics in AI at Oxford University. He is the author of *A World Without Work* and co-author (with Richard Susskind) of the bestselling *The Future of the Professions*.
10 Garry Kimovich Kasparov is a Russian chess grandmaster, former World Chess Champion, political activist and writer. https://news.nus.edu.sg/chess-grandmaster-garry-kasparov-the-next-move-in-the-ai-gambit/#:~:text=%E2%80%9CHumans%20%2B%20machines%E2%80%9D%20facing%20other,and%20machines%20to%20work%20together.
11 Deep Blue was a customised IBM RS/6000 SP supercomputer for chess-playing. It was the first computer to win a game, and the first to win a match, against a reigning world champion under regular time controls. It first played

world champion Garry Kasparov in a six-game match in 1996, where it won one, drew two and lost three games. It was upgraded in 1997, and in a six-game rematch it defeated Kasparov by winning two games and drawing three. Deep Blue's victory is considered a milestone in the history of artificial intelligence and has been the subject of several books and films.

12 https://news.nus.edu.sg/chess-grandmaster-garry-kasparov-the-next-move-in-the-ai-gambit/#:~:text=%E2%80%9CHumans%20%2B%20machines%E2%80%9D%20facing%20other,and%20machines%20to%20work%20together.

13 Sven Magnus Øen Carlsen is a Norwegian chess grandmaster. Carlsen is a five-time World Chess Champion, five-time World Rapid Chess Champion and the reigning eight-time World Blitz Chess Champion.

14 NLP stands for Natural Language Processing – a field at the intersection of linguistics, computer science and artificial intelligence. It focuses on enabling computers to understand, interpret, generate and interact using human language.

15 Predictive analytics is a type of data analytics that uses historical data, statistical algorithms and machine learning techniques to predict future outcomes or behaviours.

16 Generative AI refers to a category of artificial intelligence systems designed to create new content, such as text, images, music, videos or even code, that is similar to what a human might produce.

17 Google's Sycamore is a quantum processor developed by Google's Quantum AI team. It is one of the most advanced quantum computers built to date.

18 Some people refer to the science and the art of project management.

19 DeepMind is an artificial intelligence (AI) research lab that was founded in 2010 in London and acquired by Google (now Alphabet Inc.) in 2014. It is one of the world's leading AI research companies and has played a major role in advancing the field of artificial intelligence.

20 Elon Musk is a billionaire entrepreneur, engineer and inventor known for founding and leading multiple high-profile technology companies. He is one of the most influential and often controversial figures in the tech and business world. https://www.businessinsider.com/elon-musk-killer-robots-will-be-here-within-five-years-2014-11

21 Dean Kamen is an American inventor, entrepreneur and advocate for science and technology.

22 Jensen Huang is a Taiwanese American entrepreneur, engineer and the co-founder, president and CEO of NVIDIA Corporation, one of the world's most influential technology companies. He is widely recognised as a visionary leader in graphics processing, AI and accelerated computing. https://www.gsb.stanford.edu/insights/jensen-huang-how-use-first-principles-thinking-drive-decisions

23 Peter Brian Taylor – get it?

24 Yes, this is a ChatGPT summation – in *The Lazy Project Manager* everyone loved the 'Quick Tips to Productive Laziness' and this is just an AI empowered version of that – why not!

Chapter 2

Long live the managed project

2.1 Hail the conquering heroes (of the past)

Grab that safety rail and keep your hands inside the vehicle at all times because here comes the (respectful) history of project management in less than sixty seconds...

1. Ancient Beginnings: Massive human mega-constructions like the astonishing Egyptian Pyramids (~2600 BCE) and mystical Stonehenge (~2000 BCE) showcase early primitive but informal project management practices.[1]
2. Industrial Revolution (18th to 19th centuries): Complex and groundbreaking engineering ambitions (railroads, factories and the like) required systematic planning and coordination, which laid the foundations for modern project methods.
3. Scientific Management (Early 1900s): Frederick Taylor's Scientific Management[2] and Henry Gantt's Gantt Chart[3] (1910s) introduced structured scheduling and task optimisation to the project world.
4. World War II Project Complexity: Programmes like the Manhattan Project[4] and military logistics advanced techniques for managing large-scale and high-risk projects driven by critical time demands.
5. Critical Path Method[5] (CPM) and PERT[6] (1950s): Developed to manage interdependent activities with complex timelines, these methods became cornerstones of scheduling.
6. Founding of IPMA (1965): Originally called INTERNET (International Network of Project Management Associations), IPMA was created in Europe to promote project management as a profession globally.
7. Founding of PMI (1969): The Project Management Institute was established in the US to advance standards, certification and research in project management.

DOI: 10.4324/9781003672357-2

8. Publication of PMBOK Guide (1987): PMI released *A Guide to the Project Management Body of Knowledge*, formalising terminology, processes and knowledge areas.
9. Agile and Iterative Methods Emerge (1990s to 2000s): The Agile Manifesto[7] (2001) and frameworks like Scrum, Kanban and Lean revolutionised adaptive project delivery.
10. *The Lazy Project Manager*[8] published (2009): The bestselling proponent of smart working (productive laziness) from Peter Taylor.
11. Digital Transformation and AI (2010s to present): Cloud collaboration tools, predictive analytics and artificial intelligence are transforming planning, tracking and decision-making in project management worldwide.

It is impossible to underplay the value and contribution to society as a whole that project management has played (and will continue to play) in delivering an unimaginable number of projects of change across a vast range of industries and impacting millions (if not billions) of people.

And just as a side note here, anyone who peddles the 'projects keep failing' anti-project management argument, just look at the huge numbers of infrastructure projects, health projects, space projects, natural world projects and so on. And then reflect and keep quiet. No, not all projects deliver, but most do.

2.2 Today is a dinosaur

All that is history, but now is the start of the future.

I am now keen to progress with exploring the end of human leadership in project management. Are you ready for this?

Big idea: Big challenge: Big change.

My declaration is this:

In the 2035[9] future, the concept of 'human leadership' in project management will become generally obsolete (for advanced thinking organisations and therefore for the most successful organisations). Instead of humans overseeing or guiding AI in a collaborative partnership type role, leadership itself will be fully assumed by AI systems, programmed with complex ethical decision-making algorithms and an innate understanding of human goals, emotions and motivations.

An AI system capable of 'managing' humans.

With AI evolving to such a level where it can understand not only the 'how' of project delivery (the mechanics if you like) but also the 'why' (the value, the purpose, enveloped by ethical considerations and cultural values, driven by stakeholder interests etc.), then (most) human leadership will become redundant.

AI, guided by deep learning algorithms, will take on the role of 'ethical decision-maker', of 'strategic visionary' and of 'relationship manager' across all levels of project orchestration within an organisation.

In fact, the more complex the project landscape, the more likely this is to happen.

Now for those of you who are avid readers of my work, or who at least have read *The Lazy Project Manager*, you know I do like to use dinosaurs as a form of visual representation, but in this instance, I can't think of one.

Except that today's project management is the 'dinosaur' and AI is the 'asteroid' maybe?[10]

With the exception that the 'asteroid' is not just malevolent and destructive in this case but it is a brilliant creative, hyper-productive and genius level beast for good.

> *If you want to get a brontosaurus from 'A' to 'B', you ride the dinosaur – you don't carry it'.*
>
> (Peter Taylor)[11]

It's a fun and memorable way to illustrate working smarter: Use what you have instead of trying to over-exert an outdated way.

2.3 What is this invisible idea anyway?

Right, post impact of the AI asteroid and with the world of project management reeling with the after-effects what is left?

Figure 2.1 Dinosaur.

A world of the 'Invisible Project Manager' with AI systems that silently, seamlessly manage workflows, timelines and resources.

Well, that is my proposition anyway.

Speculative? To some degree.

Scary? Depends on your attitude to rapid change.

Exciting? I certainly think so (but of course I could be in a minority of one, and towards the end of my career).

The switch this will bring about is the focus on the project, and only the project, and a reduction in the importance of the project manager.

2.3.1 *A working definition*

The 'Invisible Project Manager' is my idea[12] that the future of project management will be AI-powered, largely automated and will eliminate the need for a traditional, visible, human project manager. Instead of a single named individual coordinating the work, a blend of intelligent systems (algorithms, bots and predictive analytics) will handle almost all of the planning, the monitoring, the reporting and those tricky stakeholder engagement tasks, all behind the scenes and without emotion or fuss.

At its core, the concept argues that:

- Project management will become a capability and no longer be a role.
- The function of managing scope, schedule, cost and risk (etc. etc. etc.) is instead embedded in platforms and workflows, rather than assigned to a person with the title of 'project manager' (or leader, or director or whatever).
- Project management is always ongoing through continuous data collection and analysis, replacing the current periodic status updates we all live with.

AI will orchestrate all delivery seamlessly and dynamically:

- Machine learning will forecast delays and reallocate resources automatically and purely objectively.
- Intelligent assistants will generate plans, update schedules, assign tasks and even write reports in natural language (and multiple languages).

Human oversight will become exception-based:

- Humans need only intervene when AI cannot resolve an ambiguity or when judgement, ethics or creative problem-solving are needed (and this will be an increasingly less demand as the AI technology self-learns).
- Instead of chasing updates, humans will review AI recommendations and then approve or override them as necessary (and this too will occur increasingly less as the AI technology self-learns).

Stakeholder engagement is digitally mediated:

- Chatbots and AI agents will then handle (mostly) all routine communications, reminders and escalations.
- And real-time dashboards will keep all stakeholders informed without those tedious and time-consuming manual reporting cycles (which are mostly ignored anyway).

The project manager is now effectively invisible:

- There is no single point of visible control as the coordination will now happen in the background, quietly, 24-7/367.
- What used to require hundreds or thousands of hours of project management effort per project will inevitably become an automated service.

In short, *The Invisible Project Manager* represents a shift from:

- The project manager is the central hub of project management.
- To an integrated, AI-enabled utility.

It's an evolution beyond simply digitising project management tools as this is about removing the visible human project manager layer altogether, creating a self-driving, self-healing system that manages projects faster, more consistently and more scalably than a human alone ever could achieve.

CHATPBT

Hold on to your hats indeed – project management didn't just appear fully formed one day when someone invented a Gantt Chart. We've been at this game since the Egyptians stacked up a few million limestone blocks to make a nice pointy tomb.

Fast forward past the Industrial Revolution's railways and smokestacks, then into the early 20th century, when clever folks like Frederick Taylor and Henry Gantt decided work needed to be measured, charted and generally bossed about scientifically.

World War II supercharged complexity – think Manhattan Project, with rather higher stakes than your average IT upgrade – spawning Critical Path and PERT in the 1950s.

The 1960s gave us IPMA and PMI to put a professional badge on our collective efforts, and by the late 1980s, PMBOK arrived to formalise everything (and yes, to ensure bedtime reading for generations of PMs). Agile, Scrum and Kanban swept in to shake things up (and confuse people who liked their Gantt Charts neat), before my own modest contribution – The Lazy Project Manager *– encouraged everyone to work smarter, not harder.*

Today, AI and digital tools are quietly revolutionising how we plan and deliver, but let's be clear: For thousands of years, project management has delivered wonders big and small that have shaped our civilisation. So next time someone smugly tells you 'Projects always fail', feel free to point them to the Pyramids – and then suggest they keep quiet.

Notes

1 These are the common references but in reality, the oldest known human mega-constructions include Göbekli Tepe in Turkey, dating back to the 10th millennium BCE, and the Blinkerwall, a submerged structure in the Baltic Sea, potentially constructed by Palaeolithic hunters between 11,700 and 9,900 years ago. These structures represent some of the earliest monumental constructions and highlight the sophisticated engineering capabilities of early human societies.
2 Frederick Winslow Taylor is known as the 'Father of Scientific Management'; his theory aimed to improve economic efficiency, especially labour productivity, by applying scientific methods to analyse and optimise work processes. This involved breaking down complex tasks into smaller, more manageable parts and optimising factory layouts.
3 Henry Gantt's Gantt Chart is a visual tool used in project management to represent a project schedule. It displays tasks on a horizontal timeline, with bars indicating the duration and dependencies between tasks. While Gantt is credited with popularising the chart, a similar concept, the 'harmonogram' was developed earlier by Karol Adamiecki.
4 The Manhattan Project was a top-secret US-led research and development project during World War II aimed at creating the first atomic bombs. It involved collaboration with the United Kingdom and Canada.
5 The Critical Path Method (CPM) is a project management technique used to identify the sequence of tasks that are crucial for project completion and determine the shortest possible project duration. It helps in scheduling, resource allocation and risk management by pinpointing the critical path – the longest sequence of dependent activities.
6 PERT is a statistical project management tool used to analyse and represent the tasks involved in completing a project, especially those with uncertain timelines.
7 The Agile Manifesto is a document that identifies 4 key values and 12 principles that its authors believe software developers should use to guide their work.
8 Productive laziness is a concept from Peter Taylor that suggests efficiency can be achieved by strategically minimising effort and focusing on high-impact

tasks, rather than striving for constant, strenuous activity. It's about working smarter, not harder, by identifying and prioritising what truly matters and automating or delegating less important tasks.

9 OK. So yes, I picked a date ten years out from the writing of this book, but you have to put a placeholder somewhere, and 2035 is the one I picked. Sure, I could be five years out either way, but it will happen; I am increasingly convinced.

10 The most widely accepted theory for the extinction of dinosaurs is the asteroid impact theory, also known as the Alvarez hypothesis. This theory proposes that a large asteroid, estimated to be 10–15 kilometres in diameter, struck the Earth approximately 66 million years ago, triggering a mass extinction event known as the Cretaceous-Paleogene (K-Pg) extinction.

11 Peter Taylor, *The Lazy Winning Project Manager* (Routledge, UK, December 2024).

12 This is my theory and this is what it is... Monty Python.

Chapter 3

The great delusion

Why we fell in love with project managers

3.1 The super project manager

I have, many times in my presentations, joked about the 'uniform' for project managers (PM) – cape, underpants, capital P etc. – and projected the image of the project manager as some heroic form. 'Oh look' says everyone in the office as the superhero clothed PM strides past 'Everything will be OK now; the project manager has arrived' [Check out the appendices for the full version].

From the birth of modern corporations to the rise of the mighty technology giants, project managers have become the indispensable linchpins of progress. We trusted them to be the super glue between strategy and the execution of that strategy. To be the voice of reason amid a sea of discordant chaos. To be the guardians of milestones and quality. And to sort all the crap out as and when it came flying out of the fan.

But somewhere along the way, perhaps our affection for project managers has grown into something closer to blind devotion, reaching a point of great delusion that they alone could guarantee success. Maybe that is an unfair comment, but from the early days of my career of 'what is a project manager' to today, when it is more of 'just give it to a project manager' file and forget.

3.2 We don't need another hero

So let us explore why we have reached the state of absolute belief in project managers and why they seem to be the only answer.

- The comfort of control
  - Humans crave predictability and do not seek chaos or confusion or instability, as such project managers promised us all order with timelines, milestones, budgets, resource plans, RAID[1] logs and much

DOI: 10.4324/9781003672357-3

Figure 3.1 Super PM.

more. In a world swirling with uncertainty,[2] they made us feel like someone (anyone) was in charge and therefore in control.

And sometimes, feeling like someone was in control was more important than someone actually being in control. It helped us all sleep better at night.

- The myth of the neutral facilitator
    - We fooled ourselves that project managers (or all mighty project management profession) were neutral brokers of progress, being dispassionate and unbiased, being committed only to the greater good. Objective in all that matters.

But project managers are only human and come with their own personal (inbuilt and learned) biases, their own ambitions and, of course, many limitations. The myth of the perfectly objective project manager has rarely, if ever, matched reality.

- The cult of certifications
  - Over decades, an entire ecosystem of certifications, methodologies and process frameworks emerged such as the PMP[3] from PMI, the PRINCE2[4] ones, a host of Agile,[5] a smattering of Lean,[6] plus good old Six Sigma.[7]

It seems for some people the more letters after your name, the more credible you must be. Our fascination with credentials made us equate a snazzy certificate in a frame on our office wall with competence.[8]

- The hero narrative
  - We all love stories with heroes. In our project story, the project manager has become the mighty protagonist who swoops in to rescue failing initiatives, with all around them swooning or craving to be them.

In reality this narrative left little room to recognise that successful projects are usually the product of a great team and collective effort and not the triumph of a lone figure (this is the pioneer versus cavalry concept).

- The illusion of accountability
  - Appointing a single person project manager (albeit working in supposed partnership with a project sponsor who knew what the hell they were doing) made it easy to pinpoint who was 'responsible' (occasionally this title was switched to 'scapegoat', but let's not dwell on that miscarriage of justice.

But assigning blame (or credit) to one role often obscures the systemic factors that make or break a project. Just take a quick Google search on project failure and you will find contributing factors such as unclear goals, cultural dysfunction, unrealistic expectations, lack of resources, failed leadership and more. I have never seen a project fail just because of just one person.

- The false promise of transformation
  - Many organisations believed that hiring a 'good' project manager was an automatic ticket to transformation success; they thought wrong.

It was just a convenient delusion, why? Because it deferred responsibility from leaders, teams and sponsors who were supposed to be bringing about this 'transformation', but in reality, had no clue how to do it.

- The professionalisation of project management
  - Over time, project management has become a profession in its own right, with career paths, many associations and industry lobbies.

All good intentions in the early days and with much of value created or shared as a result, but this professionalisation solidified the idea that projects could not be successful without a dedicated project manager.

And to be perfectly clear, when I speak of my 'profession' of project management it has nothing to do with the associations but rather with the multitude of change leaders who are not actively affiliated with major project management associations.[9]

- The technology mirage
  - Ironically, as collaboration tools and AI-powered platforms proliferated, we doubled down on project management as a job description rather than questioning whether technology should shift how we organise and deliver work.

Hence the writing of this book!

Times are changing for sure, and there is no longer an option to keep on keeping on.

It's time to reimagine how projects succeed by empowering teams, leveraging brilliant new technology and building cultures where delivery is a shared responsibility.

Because the best projects don't really need a hero.

The best projects just need clarity, together with trust, and a healthy dollop of collaboration.

It is no longer about the project manager; it is about the project.

3.3 The cloak of invisibility

In my well-known 'keynote' on productive laziness, based on my first book *The Lazy Project Manager*, I start by declaring that we have a real problem in project management.[10] We are, or we certainly were, it seemed to me all those years ago, somewhat invisible.

I joked that when you go to project management parties, you play this game (come on, you've been to hundreds of those, haven't you?).

OK, the game – find a project manager and get them to answer two questions with the first thing that comes into their head. OK, here goes.

- Q1: What are you?
- A1: I'm a project manager.

- Q2: What do you do?
- A2: I manage projects.

Result is – well, nothing; I am absolutely no better off understanding what you do than a minute ago.

Sigh.

The trouble is that if you actually try to get a more detailed answer then it can rapidly turn into a rehash of a body of knowledge (and that will bore the **** out of everyone at the party, and you will be left all alone in the kitchen contemplating your sad existence of a life).

Check out an article I did many years ago on explaining project management to an alien https://www.linkedin.com/pulse/alien-project-management-peter-taylor/

Of course, I now believe that this will all change and there may, in fact, no longer be project management parties to go to and the conversation/game will be very different.

In *The Invisible Project Manager* era, now if you go to a project management party there are no people, perhaps just some ambient music coupled with mood lighting, and maybe a dashboard floating in the air displaying 'Project Portfolio Health currently at 94% Green'.

You look around and finally spot someone in the corner.

- Q1: What are you?
- A1: I'm an outcome architect.
- Q2: What do you do?
- A2: I translate strategic intent into autonomous workflows and monitor emergent value patterns driving to outcome success.

Sorry, what was that?

Apparently, in this brave new AI-empowered project world, there are no longer any traditional project managers (at least not the clipboard-wielding, meeting-minuting, task-juggling variety from the archaic annals of history). Instead, there are orchestrators, there are narrators, and maybe value whisperers [we will explore the new AI PM roles later in the book so please be patient, we are on a journey here]. And the actual 'doing' of project management [project manager is, after all, a verb and not a noun], well that's done invisibly, in the background, by AI systems that make Jira[11] and Gantt Charts look like ancient relics.

Try asking one of these AI-driven tools what it does and it replies:

- *'I synthesise cross-functional dependencies, manage dynamic risk matrices, and realign deliverables with shifting strategic priorities in real time'.*

Translation (yep, I needed one as well) I do everything a project manager used to do, but I do it faster, much quieter and without needing coffee or a mid-afternoon nap.

So now, the party game isn't 'find a project manager', it's more like 'spot the human'.

Because in this future, project management has become 'invisible'.

CHATPBT

It has been joked (to be fair by the author mostly) that project managers come with a superhero uniform – cape, underpants on the outside and a giant capital P on the front of their shirt – striding into offices to save the day while everyone sighs in relief.

Over time, this heroic myth has hardened into an unhelpful delusion: that a single project manager, armed with a Gantt Chart and a string of certifications, can single-handedly guarantee success. We fell in love with the comforting illusion of control, the myth of the neutral facilitator, and the thrill of having a designated scapegoat when things went pear-shaped. We bought into the cult of credentials and the promise that hiring 'the right' PM would magically transform everything.

But in reality, no number of framed certificates or tidy RAID logs can mask the fact that projects thrive through collective effort, not individual heroics. As technology reshapes how we work, it's time to ditch the cape and embrace a new mindset: The best projects don't need a hero – they need clarity, trust, shared ownership and the courage to let go of old myths.

Notes

1 A RAID log is a project management tool that tracks Risks, Assumptions, Issues and Dependencies. It helps project managers proactively identify and manage potential problems throughout the project lifecycle. The log is typically a table or spreadsheet with columns for each RAID element, allowing for detailed tracking and management of each item. I have added the explanation for completeness, but it you did need that explaining, then we are all in trouble.

2 We all know about the VUCA world today. VUCA stands for Volatility, Uncertainty, Complexity and Ambiguity. It's a framework used to describe the turbulent and unpredictable nature of the modern world, particularly in business and leadership contexts. The term originated in the late 1980s at the US Army War College to describe the post-Cold War environment and was later adopted to describe the business landscape.
3 The PMP, or Project Management Professional, certification is a globally recognised credential offered by the Project Management Institute (PMI).
4 PRINCE2, which stands for PRojects IN Controlled Environments, is a structured project management methodology widely recognised and used globally. It provides a framework for managing projects effectively by breaking them down into manageable stages.
5 Agile certifications validate a professional's knowledge and skills in Agile methodologies, particularly useful for those working in software development, IT, operations, marketing and HR. These certifications demonstrate proficiency in Agile principles, frameworks like Scrum and practical application of Agile practices. Popular certifications include those from Scrum Alliance, Project Management Institute (PMI) and Scaled Agile, covering roles like Scrum Master, Product Owner and Agile coach.
6 Lean certification validates an individual's knowledge and application of lean principles, methodologies and tools. It is offered by various organisations, and the specific requirements and levels of certification can vary. Common levels include Lean Practitioner, Lean Leader and Lean Expert/Master.
7 Six Sigma is a data-driven methodology focused on process improvement, aiming to reduce defects and variability in business processes. It utilises a structured approach, often DMAIC (Define, Measure, Analyse, Improve, Control), to identify and eliminate the root causes of problems, leading to increased efficiency, customer satisfaction and cost savings.
8 I have removed all of mine, some time ago as well.
9 While a precise global percentage is difficult to determine due to varying definitions and data availability, it is estimated that a relatively small percentage of project professionals are formally affiliated with a project management association. A significant number of project professionals may not be members of any specific organisation, while others may belong to multiple associations.
10 Many other keynotes are available – maybe check out https://thelazyprojectmanager.com/speaking
11 Jira is a project management tool developed by Atlassian. It's used for planning, tracking, releasing and supporting software, but can also be adapted for various project management needs. Jira is particularly popular for agile development, offering features like Kanban and Scrum boards and workflow customisation.

Chapter 4

Software ate the tools, now it's eating the role

4.1 Disclaimer

I am now going to reference some tools and technology purely for the purpose of the narrative. That's it. Nothing more.

Please be very clear these are in no way personal recommendations. A number of the tools I do have experience of, but some I don't; therefore, I am referencing them only to support my argument of change.

OK, I think that is clear; we can now move on. Thank you for your indulgence.

> *Software is eating the world.'*
>
> (Marc Andreessen)[1]

4.2 We have been on the road for some time

In the early decades of digital project management, software emerged that offered effectively an assistant, a helpful sidekick or project buddy to the human project manager.

It all began with the digitisation of some of the typical project management tools:

- Gantt Charts moved from whiteboards to screens.
- Risk logs shifted from paper to spreadsheets and then to cloud-based spreadsheets.
- Status reports became automated dashboards with exciting colouring and sometimes animation of trending.

Project management software promised all of us time savings and great productivity improvements, but it never seemed to even remotely suggest replacing the project manager.

DOI: 10.4324/9781003672357-4

For years, the assumption was that these tools, this technology, pre-AI and early-AI, would merely augment human judgement, not supplant it.[2] The digital dance as I have previously described.

But today, right now, we are witnessing (if you are paying attention that is and not ignoring it or putting your head in a bucket) something truly unprecedented. AI software is no longer just eating the tools; it's starting to consume the role itself.

The AI transformation hasn't happened overnight of course.[3] It is the result of decades of incremental innovation and, probably, millions of hours of technology investment.

In the early 2000s, project management platforms like Microsoft Project[4] and Primavera[5] made planning more efficient but remained (very) difficult to master. A project manager still had to wrangle the software, manually update schedules and manually interpret progress while making decisions and updating it (to do it all again in the next cycle).

Cloud platforms like Basecamp,[6] Asana,[7] and Jira[8] then successfully lowered the barrier to entry (cost and effort) while adding collaborative features and true real-time updates. These tools became indispensable for many organisations and for individual users, but they were still just tools, just passive systems needing and waiting for human input, without which nothing happened, of course.

What came next was the beginning of the world-changers enjoying the beauty of the integration of machine learning, together with natural language processing and with an enticing topping of predictive analytics. Through these technological innovations, project management software evolved (rapidly) from mere static repositories into (hyper) active agents. Instead of merely recording tasks the AI-powered platforms could now start to recommend actions, forecast delays and even draft critical communications to stakeholders.

Software stopped being a passive ledger and began to behave more like an assistant project manager. We had reached the stage of the digital (dancing) assistant. A point at which many (me included originally) thought we would happily rest and just enjoy the 'machine' dealing with all the boring repetitive crap.

Consider for a moment the modern AI-infused or powered project management platform.

- When a delivery milestone slips, it doesn't just flag the issue, oh dearie me no, it proposes mitigation strategies, probably with options and outcome gradings.
- If a project team member falls behind for some reason, the system doesn't just sigh and shrug its virtual shoulders, of course not. Instead,

it predicts downstream effects and reallocates resources as needed, perhaps alerting someone to have a quiet word.

- If the client/stakeholder/sponsor requests a change, nobody gets into the mood and starts shouting about extra cost and wasting of time (well maybe that will still happen in the human world), but in the calm, objective, neutral world of AI, what will happen is the models will assess the scope impact, then update budgets and finally suggest a new timeline with all the adjustments incorporated.

These capabilities are no longer theoretical; in fact they are already available in leading SaaS[9] platforms, and adoption is growing rapidly.

4.3 A case in point

I am not going to go into a lot of detail on case studies here. Go and find some yourself; they are growing all the time and, certainly by the time this book is published, there will be even more amazing productivity examples.

Instead, here is a snapshot of some declared right now:[10]

These *diverse and documented successes* show how AI-driven insights, automation and risk prediction are delivering real measurable gains, with everything from cost savings and significant efficiency boosts to improved delivery and improved compliance.[11]

Here's another that may register with you since it involves a platform most of us have used at some point.

Company	AI Use Case	Key Outcome
MIGSO-PCUBED	Predictive project success modeling	96 % accuracy, 18 % cost savings
Mortenson + Doxel	Site monitoring via computer vision	38 % boost in productivity
Microsoft	Workflow analytics & meeting summarization	+25 % completion, −30 % admin overhead
Siemens	Risk prediction from historical data	40 % risk reduction
Turner Construction	Early risk identification	12 % reduction in overruns
Vinci Group	Automated compliance document checks	40 % less paperwork time
Asana	AI virtual teammates	25 % less project lag
Nestlé	Production waste tracking	87 % reduction in waste

Figure 4.1 AI use cases.

On eBay,[12] every single year, 60 million disputes arise, and they're resolved online without any traditional lawyers using what's known as an E-mediation[13] platform. So just to put the 60 million in context, that is 40 times the number of civil claims that are filed in the entire English and Welsh justice system. It's three times the number of lawsuits filed in the entire US legal system.

They're resolved on this one website every year with no traditional lawyers involved. A great example of actually taking the human to human (direct) out of the process speeds things up.

And Amazon is another one. I have just checked (and it is pretty scary when you do this) that over the last 10 years I have placed 2,458 orders through Amazon. I would guestimate that I have had perhaps issues with 2% of the orders placed, so say 50 orders in total and every single one was resolved to my satisfaction. Refunds, returns, replacements and in one special case a compensation (small but appreciated) and in none did I ever talk to a human.

Now, with nearly 5 billion orders per year, a similar 2% having some issue is a really big number, but no one I know has a big problem with the company. I am sure there will be someone reading this who has a real issue that has not been resolved, but the numbers generally speak for themselves in the fact that humans are out of the equation and, in the vast majority of cases, all is well as a result.

4.4 Now it has a taste for high order tasks as well

The bigger story right now is how these (AI) intelligent systems are absorbing the higher-order tasks that were once the sole domain of the human project manager:

- Coordination
- Decision-making
- Communication
- Negotiation

This is the pivot I have recently come to recognise. The point break that will swing away from the human project manager towards the AI (Invisible) project manager.

Historically all these were considered the 'soft skills' that no software could replicate. This was perhaps the 'art' in project management as opposed to the 'science' of project management.

But that belief is crumbling under the weight of rapid and astonishing innovation (at least it is with myself and quite a few others).

For example, AI can now draft empathetic updates to stakeholders delightfully tuned to their individual personalities and within the parameters of their preferred communication styles.

I use LLMs[14] daily now, and I have learnt that they can attune to the persona that I am currently representing. For example, am I asking as 'Peter Taylor, The Lazy Project Manager'? or am I asking as 'Peter Taylor the VP of a global PMO'? or am I asking as just 'Peter Taylor'? It varies the output significantly and it is amazing to experience (and it is getting better every day).

Sentiment analysis identifies when a client or team member is growing frustrated by something, prompting preemptive interventions. In complex programmes, predictive analytics bring to the surface hidden dependencies, revealing issues before even the most seasoned project manager could detect them. This is real, I worked with a startup that focused on team dynamics, and it was powerful to see in action.[15]

These are not mere enhancements, but they are capabilities that fundamentally and comprehensively challenge the need for a 'human in the loop',[16] or at least a human-in-the-loop on a regular basis.

This raises an uncomfortable question for our profession.

If software can do so much, then what on earth is going to be left for the project manager to do?

Enter 'The Invisible Project Manager'.

You might, and many will, argue that humans will always be required for judgement calls, leadership and navigating ambiguity, dealing with moralistic issues and managing other humans.

There is some truth to that.

But it's also true, I believe, that these conceptual boundaries are shifting faster than expected. In fact, the Gartner 'shock' notice of the 80% loss of project management tasks to AI is, in the near future reality, a conservative figure.

The concept of 'judgment' is being redefined as machine learning systems ingest vast datasets of past projects in order to predict the most effective decisions. Leadership too can be partially automated through nudging behaviours (software prompting teams to act, acknowledge and stay engaged). Even ambiguity can be modelled statistically with simulations quantifying uncertainty and recommending the most probable/sensible/logical[17] course of action.

In other words, what we used to consider uniquely human is now being un-uniquely (is that even a word) digitised and scaled.

None of this is to say that project managers are immediately becoming obsolete. Of course, this will take some time, and we know that organisations will move at varying speeds, with (b)leading edge and laggards. But we are, without doubt, moving towards a future where the project manager's role will be radically transformed.

The project manager will become less of a user of and more a steward of such automation (designing workflows, or training models and validating AI outputs). The human then becomes then the supervisor of the 'Invisible Project Manager' with the AI platform running silently in the background, doing the job, 24/7, 365, without deviation, distraction and objectively.

This evolution parallels what happened in other fields.

- In finance, traders were replaced by algorithms that could process market data faster and with fewer biases.
- In manufacturing, production lines became highly automated, with humans overseeing exceptions.
- In transportation, self-driving (autonomous) systems increasingly handle the mechanics of navigation.
- In health diagnoses of common issues, it is increasingly possible, and in some cases, not only faster but more accurate.

Project management is just on the same trajectory, though many have been somewhat slow to acknowledge it (and the powers that be – #projectassociations – perhaps feel rather (financially) threatened by it all).

> As machines become more intelligent, the question becomes not what can machines do, but what should they do.
>
> (Satya Nadella)[18]

For project managers who want to remain relevant (and employed/of value) then the imperative is pretty clear: Evolve your skill set from managing tasks to managing the ecosystem.

Critics of this trend could argue that AI lacks the moral compass[19] and ethical nuance to lead projects responsibly, and this is very true, today. But it is also true that such ethical frameworks can easily be encoded into the AI systems, and with that governance models can be built to keep them aligned with our defined human values.

And here is the biggy. Whatever we/you as individuals think or feel, the organisations we work for will always choose automation for speed, for consistency, and for that lovely thing, cost efficiency, even if it means redefining what 'leadership' looks like.

In the end, the phrase 'software ate the tools' feels almost quaint compared to what is really happening now. We are witnessing the gradual consumption of the role itself; the rise of 'The Invisible Project Manager' doesn't look like a human, it doesn't sit in meetings or sign off on budgets in the traditional sense, and it doesn't get depressed or distracted or tired or stressed or need another coffee/bio break. It just is and it just does.

If this feels unsettling, it should.

Disruption always does.

The future of project management will not be defined by those who cling to the old tools and old ways. It will be defined by those who embrace the concept of 'The Invisible Project Manager', partnering with it to create something better than either human or machine could achieve alone.

4.5 Investment beyond history

And just in case you have any doubts about where this whole AI journey is heading (and at what speed), well just reflect on this for a moment.

> The US's largest companies have spent 2025 locked in a competition to spend more money than one another, lavishing $155bn on the development of artificial intelligence, more than the US government has spent on education, training, employment and social services in the 2025 fiscal year so far.

This was an extract from *The Guardian*[20] on Big Tech spending on AI (August 2025).

And there will be more.

> Big Tech firms Amazon (AMZN), Alphabet (GOOGL, GOOG), Microsoft (MSFT), and Meta (META) reported that they were set to spend as much as a cumulative $364 billion in their respective 2025 fiscal years, driven by their investments in AI, up from their prior estimates of around $325 billion.

So reported Yahoo!/Finance[21] at the same time.

Pretty astonishing numbers, I am sure you will agree, and at an investment level never seen before in history.

Now, I'm no economist, but even I can see what this means. This isn't investment as usual; this is investment beyond anything seen before in history. We're witnessing a paradigm shift where AI isn't just a buzzword; it's the foundation of future business strategy, albeit at least for those with the deepest pockets.

We're not just accelerating into an AI-powered future; we're being rocketed into it at breakneck speed. This level of spending tells me two things:

- AI will be embedded into every aspect of enterprise life, from customer service bots to CEO-level decision-making tools.
- And more provocatively (for this reading audience perhaps) the age of human project managers may well be numbered, at least in their current form.

Because with this kind of financial firepower, AI isn't just going to assist project delivery; it's going to own it.

So, grab a coffee, and maybe a stiff drink (if that is your choice), and start thinking not about how to use AI but how to lead in a world where AI is the alpha partner.

4.6 A hard truth

There's a hard truth that white-collar professionals, especially those of us in project management, must confront today ideally. Our roles, as secure and intellectually valuable as they've seemed for decades, are no longer untouchable. The AI revolution isn't coming; it's already unpacking its bags in our (virtual) offices and putting its own digital potted plant on the shelf.

One of the most compelling arguments I've come across recently concerns the distinction between jobs and tasks. And this, I believe, is the first big reason we all need to take the rise of AI seriously. You see, when you break down a job (any job) into the individual tasks that make it up, then things begin to look very different. This isn't just anecdotal. McKinsey & Company took on the formidable task of analysing 820 different occupations in the US labour market and produced some fascinating findings.[22]

They found that only 5% of jobs could be fully automated with current technologies (now to be fair this was in 2017 so the landscape will have changed somewhat by now). But even though only a handful of complete jobs can be fully automated, a staggering 60% of those jobs consist of tasks and 30% or more of which could be automated. Think about this totally honestly in regard to your day-to-day work. Think of your '9 to 5' in the shape of tasks versus non-tasks.

So, what does this mean for us in project delivery?

It means that while your title might survive intact, the substance of your day-to-day work could be done faster, cheaper and often better by machines.

- Scheduling: Automated and more comprehensive.
- Risk modelling: Done through predictive analytics.
- Status reporting: Delivered through real-time updated dashboards.

And that's really just scratching the surface, so let us go deeper.

One might argue that the remaining tasks in project management, the ones requiring creativity, stakeholder empathy and strategic judgement are perhaps safe. After all, machines can't 'think' or 'feel' right?

Well, yes and no.

The second reason white-collar workers should pay close attention to AI is precisely because we're starting to see machines performing tasks that simulate creativity, approximate judgement and even mimic empathy (just not in the human way we're used to – a bit like Deep Blue did not play chess like Kasparov).

- A large language model can generate stakeholder communication plans tailored to audience personas.
- Generative AI tools can brainstorm project risk mitigations based on industry datasets.
- And digital agents can simulate project coaching sessions in a way that, surprisingly, hits many of the right emotional notes.

The big mistake we often make is assuming that because machines don't 'feel' or 'reason' like us, they can't do what we do. But the task-level evidence says otherwise. AI doesn't need to replicate human cognition, we can see that now, it just needs to get the task done. And it's increasingly clear that it can.

For project managers and PMO leaders, this means we must think differently and not just about our roles, but about how we deliver value. The future isn't about being replaced by AI. It's about working with it, automating the predictable, amplifying the valuable and focusing human effort where it makes the biggest difference, and that, in my mind, is not in 'managing' projects.

CHATPBT

We've been on this road quite a while now.

Once upon a time, project management software was just a helpful little buddy – digitising Gantt Charts, shifting risk logs into the cloud and turning status reports into dashboards. All very nice, but nobody imagined it would dare replace the project manager. For years, the tools merely danced politely around us, augmenting our judgement without question. But here's the thing: That dance is over. AI has pulled up a chair, grabbed the choreography and is now leading.

It started innocently enough – machine learning, predictive analytics, natural language processing – all layered on top of platforms that used to simply record what we told them. Fast forward to today, and your software doesn't just track tasks; it proposes actions, reallocates resources, drafts updates in your tone of voice and spots risks you haven't even dreamed of. And yes, it's already doing the so-called 'soft stuff' – communication, coordination, decision-making – once thought to be safe from automation.

So, what's left for the project manager?

Quite a lot less than you might like to think. The role is transforming from task wrangler to ecosystem steward, overseeing an invisible AI that never sleeps, never sulks and never needs another coffee. Just as trading, manufacturing, transport and healthcare have been fundamentally reshaped by intelligent systems, project management is next in line.

Whether you find that exhilarating or unsettling, the conclusion is the same: Clinging to the old ways won't save you. Only embracing the rise of the Invisible Project Manager will.

Notes

1 Marc Andreessen is an American entrepreneur, software engineer, venture capitalist and one of Silicon Valley's most influential figures. https://www.forbes.com/sites/josipamajic/2025/05/22/software-ate-the-world-ai-ate-software-and-now-philosophy-is-eating-ai/

2 As I have already admitted, this was the theme of my first book on AI and project management, as well as my focus of work in recent years since that book came out.

3 You can read some of the evolution history of AI in my *AI and the Project Manager* book as well as easily grab a history via your favourite search engine (so last year) or your favourite large language learning model (LLM).

4 Microsoft Project is project management software developed by Microsoft. It helps project managers plan, manage and track projects by providing tools for scheduling, resource management, budget tracking and more.

5 Primavera, specifically Primavera P6, is enterprise project portfolio management software developed by Oracle. It's a robust tool used for planning, managing and executing projects, programmes and portfolios across various industries. It helps with tasks like scheduling, resource management, cost management and risk analysis.

6 Basecamp is a web-based project management and team collaboration tool designed to help teams organise work, communicate effectively and stay on top of tasks and deadlines. It's known for its user-friendly interface and is particularly well-suited for small businesses and teams.

7 Asana is a web and mobile work management platform that helps teams organise, track and manage their work. It's designed to improve team collaboration, streamline workflows and connect work to strategic goals. Essentially, it's a tool that helps teams manage projects, tasks and communication in one centralised location.

8 Jira is a project management software developed by Atlassian. It's primarily used for tracking issues, managing projects and automating workflows, particularly within software development teams. Jira is known for its flexibility and can be customised to support various project management methodologies and workflows.

9 SaaS (Software as a Service) is a cloud-based software delivery model where users access applications online via subscription without needing to install or manage them locally.

10 References being – https://aipmp.ai/transforming-project-management-with-ai-case-studies-and-insights/ and https://smartdev.com/ai-use-cases-in-project-management/ and https://neuroject.com/ai-in-project-management-case-studies/

11 I have avoided, as best I can. Any specific references to technology status as, almost certainly, by the time you read this book, they will be out of date and superseded by something way more impressive. That is the point. Tech progress is off the scale.

12 eBay Inc. is a British multinational e-commerce company based in San Jose, California, that allows users to buy or view items via retail sales through online marketplaces and websites in 190 markets worldwide.

13 E-mediation, also known as online mediation, is a form of dispute resolution where a neutral third party (the mediator) facilitates communication and negotiation between disputing parties using electronic means like video conferencing or online platforms. This allows for remote mediation, eliminating the need for physical presence.

14 An LLM (Large Language Model) is an AI system trained on vast text data to understand and generate human-like language.

15 *Team Analytics: The Future of High-Performance Teams and Project Success* – 2023 (Routledge) – Bentzy Goldman, Peter Taylor.

16 'Human-in-the-loop' (HITL) refers to a system or process where humans and machines collaborate, with humans actively participating in the decision-making and learning process of an AI or machine learning system. It's a way to combine human intelligence and expertise with the power of automation.

17 Time for a Spock quote maybe? 'Logic is the beginning of wisdom, not the end of it' and 'Insufficient facts always invite danger'. Spock, the half-Vulcan science officer from Star Trek, known for his logical and emotionless demeanour.

18 Satya Nadella is an Indian American business executive best known as the Chairman and CEO of Microsoft, one of the world's largest and most influential technology companies. He is widely credited with transforming Microsoft into a cloud-first, AI-driven and innovation-focused company after taking the helm in 2014. https://news.microsoft.com/europe/features/artificial-intelligence-needs-human-touch/#:~:text=%E2%80%9CWe%20are%20trying%20to%20teach,This%20is%20highly%20do%2Dable.

19 A set of beliefs or values that help guide ethical decisions, judgements and behaviour: An internal sense of right and wrong.

20 https://www.theguardian.com/technology/2025/aug/02/big-tech-ai-spending

21 https://finance.yahoo.com/news/big-techs-ai-investments-set-to-spike-to-364-billion-in-2025-as-bubble-fears-ease-143203885.html
22 McKinsey Global Institute, 'A future that works: Automation, employment, and productivity' https://www.mckinsey.com/~/media/mckinsey/featured%20insights/Digital%20Disruption/Harnessing%20automation%20for%20a%20future%20that%20works/MGI-A-future-that-works-Executive-summary.ashx

Chapter 5

The rise of the invisible project manager

5.1 Attacking the sacred cows

Project management is full of sacred cows.

We all know them.

These are the practices, or tools and certainly some beliefs that everyone treats as absolutely untouchable.

The trouble is, the more we cling to these assumptions, the more we distance ourselves from the reality of the now, and light years away from the future.

If project people want to stay relevant and genuinely add value (like we are supposed to do), then we need to be willing to lead a few of these cows gently to the slaughterhouse (or at least to retirement pasture if that is a preferred image for you).

Take the Gantt Chart, perhaps the most revered of all project artefacts. No kick-off meeting feels complete without a grand timeline cascading across a slide, impressing (or confusing in most cases) absolutely everyone in the room. But let us be honest, most of the time, the good old reliable Gantt Chart merely offers the comforting illusion of control and foresight in situations where neither really exists. The moment you finish the chart; well reality has already shifted. Dependencies move, priorities change, resources evaporate (or were never there in the first place), and yet we continue to update and circulate these diagrams as though their mere existence proves we are managing effectively.

Then there is the belief that methodology alone guarantees success. PRINCE2, PMBOK, the latest flavour of Agile, hybrid,[1] your choice. Many organisations act as if strict adherence to a framework will save a project that is otherwise heading for disaster (it generally won't in case you wondered since methodologies are useful tools, but they are not magic spells). When process becomes more important than purpose, we stop thinking and we lose sight of the human dynamics that actually drive outcomes.

DOI: 10.4324/9781003672357-5

Risk registers offer another example of ritual masquerading as substance. With teams dutifully listing all the hypothetical dangers from an annoying wasp through to seismic impacts, assigning scores and pretty colours and then filing the document away after an initial look of admiration. Then only to look completely surprised when problems inevitably appear. The risk register becomes a bureaucratic tick box rather than a living guide for action and we (often) pretend that listing risks is the same as preparing for them.

And of course, status reports. Every week teams rush to produce glossy updates full of green traffic lights and reassuring commentary. More often than not though, these reports are crafted to keep stakeholders comfortable rather than to tell them anything they really need to hear. This is project management theatre, and it is not project management truth.

Example: Extract for *The Lazy Project Manager*

> Reporting is not communicating. Just because you send out a report does not mean you have communicated anything of value. Too often, reports are produced because the process demands them, not because they genuinely inform or engage. Real communication requires clarity, relevance and a willingness to tell the truth, even when it is uncomfortable.

And now let's end this on a big one since perhaps the most dangerous sacred cow of all is the belief that the project manager must be the smartest person in the room! Well believe that and you are deep in some serious sacred cow shit. In reality, projects rarely fail because the team lacked process; oh no, they fail because they lacked honesty and shared understanding together with the flexibility to adapt and change. The project manager's role is to help create clarity and collective ownership and not to maintain the illusion of solitary control (a big mistake I made in my early career for sure).

Challenging these sacred cows is not about being difficult for the sake of it and it is not about being willfully disruptive. It is about freeing project management from empty rituals so it can become what it was meant to be, and that is a practical discipline focused on delivering value in uncertain conditions. If we never question our cherished habits, then we will keep repeating the same mistakes and call it best practice. Now this would be bad enough even in a non-changing project world, but here we are on the leading wave of a massive AI tsunami of change. Resistance is truly useless.

Sacred cows make great steaks,[2] but terrible strategy.

5.2 Removal of the biggest barrier to effective communication

How much of a project manager's time (add in team members, stakeholders, client and so on) is spent on communication? It is huge – 70% – 80% – 90%?

Meetings, stand-ups/sit-downs, updates/downloads, reports, more reports, even more reports, dashboards and spreadsheets, brainstorms, blue sky thinking and root cause analysis; it goes on and on.

And here we are in a wonderful global world with virtual project teams engaging resources from multiple countries and multiple cultures.

Did you know (I didn't so I had to look it up)? There are estimated to be around 7,111 living languages in the world.[3] Now, obviously, we don't interact with that huge number on a regular basis, but if you think of the common ones, then there are a handful of languages that dominate globally due to the number of native and non-native speakers (the exact number is subjective and depends on the criteria used). English, Mandarin Chinese, Hindi, Spanish and French are consistently ranked among the most dominant languages around the world.

I am very fortunate as my native (and only) language is English and this is the number common language used in business (which makes me productively lazy but through absolutely no effort on my part). Approximately 17% of the world's population speaks English, with about 1.35 billion people using the language. This includes both native speakers and those who speak it as a second language. While it's the third most spoken native language, it's the most widely spoken language overall due to its widespread use as a second language.

So, firstly, let me thank all of those non-native English speakers I have had the pleasure of working with over the years and assure you all that I did appreciate the extra effort that you had to put in, day after day.[4]

All that said, language can be a barrier with misunderstandings and confusion on meaning, especially in the more nuanced conversations. But now AI is revolutionising how we handle multiple languages through various applications like real-time translation, multilingual chatbots and AI-powered dubbing.

These technologies take advantage of natural language processing (NLP[5]) and machine learning to bridge language barriers and enhance communication across different languages. I use some of this technology right now and it is very impressive already.

Here's how AI powers multilingual solutions:

- Real-Time Translation:
  - AI-powered translation tools can instantly translate spoken or written language into multiple languages, thereby enabling seamless communication in meetings, during webinars and through customer interactions – powerful!
- Multilingual Chatbots:
  - AI Chatbots can understand and respond to customer queries in multiple languages, so providing an efficient and a very personalised customer engagement – also powerful!
- AI-Powered Dubbing:
  - AI can generate synthetic voices and translate audio content into different languages, which makes new video content accessible to a much wider audience – fast and powerful!
- Multilingual Content Creation:
  - AI can assist in generating and adapting content in multiple languages, which ensures linguistic accuracy and also cultural relevance for a group of diverse audiences – very powerful!
- AI Language Learning:
  - AI-powered language learning apps provide personalised learning experiences that help users improve their vocabulary, grammar, and correct pronunciation in a range of various languages – personally powerful!

Now all this takes communication to a level way, way beyond the capability of all, but the most special and elite of project managers (who would have to have a wide range of language skills). The 'Jo Average' project manager cannot hope to compete with the power of this type of technology but won't have to now as the tech is here.

Let's be honest at this point, project communication has always been one of the most exhausting parts of the job. Emails, teams' messages,[6] chat, IM, flying in from every direction, endless status meetings, both physical and virtual and the dreaded weekly report that seems to take hours to cobble together. None of it is very 'lazy' in the positive productive sense. But in the not-too-distant future, intelligent automation[7] (IA) is set to rescue us from this chaos.

Imagine a world where all your project communication is managed by an intelligent system that never sleeps, and never forgets, and doesn't even require coffee to stay sharp and on point. These tools will be able to monitor every communication, and every communication channel, all in real time and, as a result, ensure that the right information goes to the right people at the right time and in the right way.[8] There will be no more frantic copying and pasting updates from spreadsheets (used to so love that (not)) or worrying that you've left someone off an important distribution list (been there, done that).

Even better, these systems will understand both context and tone. For example, if a stakeholder sends a slightly tetchy query about a late deliverable, IA will pick up the nuance and respond appropriately, perhaps with a carefully worded reassurance or an escalation if needed. The end result, it will be like having your most diplomatic team member on hand 24/7.

Team conversations will also be subject to analysis to ensure that everyone's voice is truly heard (how often does that happen now?) and that any concerns or people being rather too quiet can be explored and acted upon.

Reporting, which has never been the highlight of anyone's week (oh come on, don't try to convince me you actually enjoy it), will be almost entirely automated. Rather than a person painstakingly preparing all those lovely slides and beautiful summaries, IA will pull real-time data from the project tools, generate tailored reports for different audiences and even anticipate the questions those pesky stakeholders might ask. Oh look, what do we have here, the right information going to the right people at the right time and in the right way – job done.

The result?

Communication that is accurate, that is consistent and is also, uniquely, 100% objective.

One of the most impressive aspects of intelligent automation is its predictive capability, so instead of reacting to issues after they've spiralled out of control, IA will flag potential problems early, alerting the team and proposing sensible next steps. In many cases, it will handle the routine follow-up without a human (in-the-loop) lifting a finger. That means less firefighting and more time to focus on strategic thinking.

Add in to this wondrous mix the previously mentioned automatic translation and cultural sensitivity checks will mean that everyone receives clear, appropriate messages, wherever they are. No more awkward misunderstandings or accidental offence caused by clumsy phrasing, or tired minds trying to translate into the common business language.

So, in this brave new world of project delivery, intelligent automation will do the heavy lifting of communication, working smarter, not harder. And that is exactly how it should be.

5.3 Like a beautiful butterfly

Right, the sacred cows have all been dealt with and gone off to the great big pasture in the sky, and we have seen that the biggest part of project management, namely communication, can be managed through and by artificial intelligence; then what's left to convince you that the AI project management world is about to break free from the chrysalis and emerge as a beautiful butterfly.

You know, if you think about it, AI in project management is a bit like 'The Very Hungry Caterpillar'.[9]

At first, it nibbled away at a few modest tasks such as scheduling a meeting here and generating a quick status update there. But it was never satisfied. It kept gobbling up more and more of our workload, on to juicy progress reports, then yummy risk logs, a tasty set of stakeholder communications, in fact anything it could get its algorithms around. And yes, it was still hungry.

And then, just like in the story, it wrapped itself up in a cocoon of machine learning and automation, and when it emerged, well, it was no longer just a caterpillar (gasp); it was a beautiful butterfly of intelligent project delivery.

> *When digital transformation is done right, it's like a caterpillar turning into a butterfly. But when done wrong, all you have is a really fast caterpillar.*
>
> (George Westerman,[10] MIT Sloan).

Now, AI soars above the drudgery, effortlessly handling the repetitive tasks that used to consume humans' time and energy (and sometimes the will to live). All the while, we, the productively focused lazy project managers, can sit back, sip our tea/coffee and admire how far it's come, from peckish little helper to magnificent, winged enabler of smarter, simpler project success.

The lazy project manager becomes the invisible project manager.

CHATPBT

Project management has long been burdened by sacred cows – practices and beliefs we treat as untouchable. The Gantt Chart is a prime example: a theatrical timeline that pretends to offer control but is usually out of date before the ink is dry. Methodologies like PRINCE2 or Agile are useful frameworks, but no rigid process guarantees success. When process becomes more important than purpose, we stop thinking.

Risk registers, too, are often little more than colourful lists we admire once before filing away, while status reports tend to be crafted for comfort rather than truth – project management theatre rather than real communication. And the most dangerous myth of all? That the project manager must be the smartest person in the room. In reality, success depends on honesty, shared understanding and adaptability – not solitary heroics.

Then there's communication: the most time-consuming, exhausting part of the job. With teams scattered across countries and cultures, misunderstandings are inevitable. But AI is transforming this. Real-time translation, multilingual chatbots and automated content creation are already bridging language gaps effortlessly. Intelligent automation tools will soon handle project communication end-to-end – tracking every message, generating reports and responding with nuance. No more endless copy-and-paste marathons or late-night status updates.

Even better, AI will predict problems before they escalate, ensure everyone is heard and deliver communication that is clear, consistent and culturally sensitive. This isn't about replacing project managers – it's about freeing us from drudgery so we can focus on what matters.

Imagine AI as the very hungry caterpillar of project management. It started nibbling at small tasks – scheduling, reporting – but kept consuming more. Now, wrapped in machine learning, it's ready to emerge as a butterfly of intelligent project delivery.

In this new world, the lazy (in the best sense) project manager finally gets to be productively lazy, supported by technology that never sleeps, never forgets and never needs coffee. We can let go of old rituals and instead lead with clarity and purpose.

Sacred cows make good steaks, but they're a terrible strategy. It's time to let them go and embrace smarter, simpler ways to deliver value.

Notes

1. I worked with 'GLAGILE' Gated Lean Agile and 'FRAGILE' Fixed Agile – yes, made-up names but it was how the teams tried to describe what was the path to project success.
2. Sacred cows are vegan, so no offence intended or made.
3. This number can vary slightly depending on the source and how languages and dialects are classified.
4. As my German colleague/friend tells me regularly, 'Peter, I am a non-native English speaker… slow down'.
5. NLP stands for Natural Language Processing and is a field of artificial intelligence that focuses on enabling computers to understand, interpret and generate human language.
6. Insert the smart comms tool of your choice here.

7 Intelligent automation (IA) combines artificial intelligence (AI) and robotic process automation (RPA) to automate complex tasks, improve decision-making and enhance business processes according to both IBM and Oracle. It leverages technologies like machine learning (ML) and natural language processing (NLP) to go beyond simple automation and enable systems to learn, adapt and make intelligent decisions.

8 The quote 'right information goes to the right people at the right time and in the right way' emphasizes the importance of effective communication and information dissemination, highlighting that the message, recipient, timing and method of delivery are all crucial for successful communication. This principle, often attributed to Peter Taylor, underscores that simply having the right information is not enough; it must reach the intended audience in a manner they can understand and at a time when it is most relevant.

9 *The Very Hungry Caterpillar* is a children's picture book written and illustrated by Eric Carle, first published in 1969. It tells the story of a caterpillar's voracious appetite as it eats its way through various foods before transforming into a butterfly. The book is known for its distinctive collage illustrations and die-cut pages, has been widely praised for its simple and yet engaging narrative and its depiction of growth and metamorphosis. PS: The author of this book only dreams of selling as many copies as that book!

10 George Westerman is a Senior Lecturer at the MIT Sloan School of Management and Founder of the Global Opportunity Initiative. https://www.forbes.com/councils/forbesbusinesscouncil/2022/03/11/digital-transformation-isnt-just-about-bits-and-bytes-its-about-people/

Chapter 6

A lazy personal comparison

6.1 Only being fair

It seems to me that I need to be completely fair in my argument that AI is going to take over my world, your world, the project world, and the best way that I can think of doing that is to compare my original lazy thoughts (from my 2009 book) and fully updated and enhanced in my 2024 book *The Lazy Winning Project Manager* published by Routledge.

The 'productively lazy'[1] project manager concept was (and remains) 'Work Smarter, Not Harder'[2] bearing in mind that *'Lazy does not mean stupid'*.[3]

Smart laziness. The concept of productive laziness combines intelligence with a focused approach to project management. It's about exercising efforts where they truly matter, rather than rushing around involving oneself in non-critical activities. This approach allows smart (lazy) project managers to balance life, their projects and their work effectively.

Key principles:

- Focus on the 20% of tasks that produce 80% of results.
- Delegate and empower team members.
- Streamline communication and processes.
- Anticipate and plan for potential issues.

By adopting these principles, good project managers can achieve success with less effort whilst ensuring projects are delivered on time and within budget, while maintaining a healthy work–life balance.

OK, well that is all well and good but does it apply in this new age of artificial intelligence and the concept of the fully automated project manager?

Let's see.

DOI: 10.4324/9781003672357-6

6.2 Productively lazy AI projects

The 80/20 rule: Focus on what truly matters:

'The Pareto Principle or 80/20 rule can and should be used by every smart but lazy person in their daily life.'[4]

Pareto Principle applied.

The 80/20 rule, also known as the Pareto Principle, states that 80% of consequences stem from 20% of causes. In project management, this translates to focusing on the critical 20% of tasks that yield 80% of the results.

Application in project management.	Identify and prioritise high-impact activities. Allocate resources efficiently. Streamline decision-making processes. Minimise time spent on low-value tasks.

Application in project management:

By applying this principle, project managers can maximize their productivity and project outcomes while minimizing unnecessary effort and resource allocation.

Well the 80/20 rule, also known as the Pareto Principle,[5] is not an algorithm; instead, it is a guideline or observation that suggests that roughly 80% of effects come from 20% of causes. While it can be used to inform how resources are allocated or how to prioritise tasks, it doesn't involve a specific set of instructions or a computational process like an algorithm[6] does.

But all that said, the AI project world can use this concept:

- In AI project management, the Pareto Principle (80/20 rule) helps leaders cut through complexity, prioritise wisely and deliver more with less. While AI may feel like new territory, the same timeless truth applies in that a small portion of inputs often drives the majority of outcomes.

Here are some examples of how this plays out in the 'Invisible Project Manager' world:

- Stakeholder prioritisation – 20% of stakeholders will drive 80% of the decisions and resistance. Smart project managers focus their engagement and communication efforts on this core group.
- Project risks and delays – A small number of dependencies, teams or unclear requirements typically cause the majority of project delays. AI can aid focus on identifying that 20% early and proactively managing them.
- Use case value – In enterprise AI portfolios, 20% of use cases usually deliver 80% of the business value. AI will guide teams to prioritise and deliver these high-impact initiatives first.

- Meetings and reports – 80% of project alignment comes from 20% of the key meetings and updates, 20% of the communication conducted. Avoid drowning in admin. Streamline communication around the few meetings that actually matter.
- Scope management – Projects can often suffer from over-engineering. Focusing efforts on the 20% of functionality that brings 80% of value to end-users or business stakeholders could be the guidelines for AI-driven projects to reduce this situation, the minimal viable solution or output.
- Strategic implications – Don't try to manage everything equally; instead, use Pareto thinking to prioritise features, use cases, stakeholders and risks. Deliver value early to build trust and momentum. All objectively possible with AI technology.

Be comfortable saying 'no' (or at least 'not now') to the 80% of work that offers marginal gain; this is where we should all be, and perhaps the emotionally remote and non-subjective AI project is a perfect solution to this.

Even in the fast-paced, tech-heavy world of AI, project success is still about prioritisation, clarity and focus. The Pareto Principle remains a powerful lens for managing complexity and maximising impact, all with potentially less effort.

6.3 The project lifecycle

Thick at the ends, thin in the middle.

The project 'dinosaur' concept:

'All projects are thick at one end, much, much thinner in the middle and then thick again at the far end.'[7]

Strategic effort allocation.

This concept emphasises that project managers should apply more effort and focus on the beginning and end of a project, while allowing the middle phase to run more smoothly with less direct involvement.

Project phases and effort distribution.	Initiation (Thick): Intensive planning, team building and setting clear objectives.
	Execution (Thin): Empowering the team, monitoring progress and addressing issues as needed.
	Closure (Thick): Thorough evaluation, knowledge transfer and lessons learned.

Application in project management:

By following this approach, project managers can ensure a strong foundation, smooth execution and valuable insights for future projects, all while optimising their own time and energy.

AI-driven or human-driven, it makes no difference.

The setup of the project and the close down of the project (the thick parts) require significant project leadership effort to get it right and to make it even better next time around.

The (thin) middle is still about the project team/resources with a lighter touch from the project leader.

In the AI project managed world the principles remain the same; it is just that the technology aids with the 'thick' efforts and needs, leading to a faster and more effective start-up and close-down.

In the middle, the team dynamic management and sentiment tracking technology kicks in with high collaborative communication and validation.

6.4 Manage your sponsor

Understand their expectations and power.

The sponsor management approach:

'Critical to any project's success is having a good project sponsor, but like the saying goes "you can pick your friends but you can't pick your relatives" – and the same is true of project sponsors.'[8]

Sponsor management strategy.

Understanding and managing your project sponsor is crucial for project success. This involves assessing their expectations, power base and communication preferences to tailor your approach accordingly.

Key steps in sponsor management:

- Conduct an initial meeting to clarify expectations and objectives.
- Analyse their power and influence using the power grid.
- Identify their motivations and 'what's in it for them'.
- Adapt your communication style to suit their preferences.
- Regularly update and engage them throughout the project lifecycle.

Application in project management:

By effectively managing your sponsor, you can secure necessary support, resources and decision-making authority to drive your project to success.

Right, this is big one for me and one that I have been writing about, speaking about and generally complaining about for years.

Bottom line is that while project managers are trained, certified and supported, project sponsors are frequently underprepared and lack clarity on their role, and this leads to misaligned expectations and failed projects.

In contrast, a strong and engaged sponsor is one of the most important predictors of project success, along with a great project manager, as they provide vision, authority, strategic alignment and executive-level escalation support – all the things project managers alone cannot deliver.

Sponsors who are present, supportive and communicative throughout the project (and not just figureheads or names on a PowerPoint) are the ones who truly deliver and provide value, as both sponsor visibility and active engagement are essential.

Project success is a shared responsibility between the sponsor and the project manager, and a good sponsor empowers the project manager, clears obstacles for them as needed and keeps the initiative aligned with the key business goals.

I have called for the professionalism of project sponsorship as this is a missing link in many project failures.

OK, that stated, does AI fix this?

I would say no; this is a critical 'human in the loop' activity. The AI world sponsor could definitely have a lighter touch if they are supported by intelligent project dashboards with insightful metrics and recommendations for action.

But the sponsors still need the knowledge of what the job is about.

6.5 Control project creep

Measure, manage and park ideas.

Change control:

'Project creep (as in functionality creep, feature creep, mission creep and scope creep) is a problem where the objectives of the project are put at risk by a gradual increase in overall objectives as the project progresses.'[9]

Change management tactics. Controlling project creep is essential for maintaining project scope, timeline and budget. This involves implementing a robust change management process and fostering a culture of controlled flexibility.

Strategies to manage project creep:
- Implement a clear change control process.
- Use the 'creep'o'meter'[10] to assess team members' tendencies for scope creep.
- Educate the team on the importance of scope management.
- Create a 'parking lot' for ideas that don't fit the current scope.
- Regularly review and prioritise change requests.
- Thank contributors for their ideas, even if they're not implemented.

Application in project management:

By effectively managing project creep, you can maintain focus on core objectives while still allowing for necessary adaptations and improvements.

Change control discipline is always required, regardless of your project methodological approach.

But the drift or creep is a human condition and not a 'machine' condition.

Put the definition parameters into the 'system' and it is locked and loaded. Any changes would just not happen without human interference or formal approval.

Now to be clear, this won't work for all projects, but I am addressing the common projects – not identical but typical and repeatable formatted projects of change – and not leading edge, first time, never been done before projects.

6.6 Effective communication

Tailor your approach.

Communication success:

'Effective communication is about isolating the critical information, utilising the optimum communication method for the person (or people) that you need to communicate with, and delivering that information at the appropriate time.'[11]

Tailored communication strategies. Effective project communication involves understanding your audience, choosing the right medium and delivering information at the right time. This approach minimizes misunderstandings and ensures that critical information reaches the right people.

Key communication principles:	Understand individual communication preferences. Develop a clear communication plan. Use a mix of communication methods (e.g., email, meetings, reports). Focus on delivering critical information concisely. Encourage two-way communication and feedback. Regularly assess and adjust communication strategies.

Application in project management:

By tailoring your communication approach, you can improve project clarity, team alignment, and overall project success.

We have already looked at the power of communication efficiency in the AI project world with multi-language and sentiment analysis and more.

Reduce the human-to-human communication and the volume of misinterpretations (accidental or intentional – you know that happens, a lot!) reduces.

As a result, productivity increases.

6.7 Fun and team building

Create a positive project environment.

Team dynamics:

'Without a little bit of fun in every project, the project world can be a dark and depressing place.[12]

Fostering team spirit. Incorporating fun and team-building activities into your project can significantly improve team morale, productivity and overall project success. A positive environment helps team members navigate challenges and maintain motivation throughout the project lifecycle.

Ideas for incorporating fun:

- Start meetings with icebreakers or jokes.
- Organize team-building activities or social events.
- Celebrate project milestones and team achievements.
- Encourage friendly competition or challenges.
- Create project-specific traditions or rituals.
- Use humour to diffuse tense situations (when appropriate).

Application in project management:

Remember to keep activities inclusive and respectful of all team members. By fostering a fun and positive project environment, you can enhance team cohesion, creativity and overall project performance.

This is a tougher one. I mean, can I imagine AI coming up with the 'Talk like a pirate day'[13] shenanigans that I did? Well not really, but will it need to is the right question to ask.

Already my PMO adds gamification into a lot that we do, and people do like it.

And already AI is increasingly being used to enhance team-building capabilities by automating tasks, providing data-driven insights and fostering better collaboration. For example, AI tools can analyse team dynamics; it can suggest optimal team compositions and even personalise team-building activities to boost engagement and productivity. Pretty neat.

The question of whether AI can be truly creative, though, is very complex and depends on how creativity is actually defined. While AI can generate novel and surprising outputs, and even surpass human performance in certain creative tasks, it certainly currently lacks the intrinsic motivation, consciousness and lived experiences that often drive the pinnacle of human creativity.

But for the truly creative and inspirational stuff, I guess we will still need those 'special' people.[14]

6.8 Stay calm in crisis

Filter, delegate and prioritise.

Crisis management:

'Breathe normally.'[15]

Crisis management approach. Staying calm during project crises is crucial for effective problem-solving and leadership. By adopting a systematic approach to crisis management, project managers can navigate challenges more effectively and maintain team confidence.

Crisis management steps:

- Breathe and stay calm.
- Filter: Identify the core issues and their sources.
- Delegate: Assign tasks to appropriate team members.
- Prioritise: Focus on high-impact actions first.
- Monitor: Keep track of progress and adjust as needed.

Application in project management:

By following this approach, project managers can maintain control during challenging situations, make better decisions and guide their teams towards successful resolutions.

Here we are deep, deep into the human world powered by opinions, assumptions, miscommunications (intended or otherwise) and a whole lot more.

Crisis management, or more likely issue response, is generally the result of something (someone) being wrong or missed or some such factor.

Emotions run high at these times, and therefore wouldn't the always neutral artificial intelligence project guidance just see these matters as one more step on the logical path, one further action to be taken.

And even more than that by constantly projecting future scenarios such impending issues will be less impactful because they will be spotted as 'possibilities' that much earlier.

I think the AI project world will be a calmer place with a whole lot less human-generated 'noise'.

6.9 Cultivate team love

Nurture the feel-good factor.

Team sentiment:

'A little love goes a long way and a lot of love goes much further.'[16]

Team nurturing strategies. Creating a positive team environment where members feel valued and supported is crucial for project success. This involves understanding individual needs, fostering a sense of belonging and providing appropriate recognition and support.

Ways to cultivate team love:	Understand each team member's motivations and preferences.
	Provide regular, meaningful feedback and recognition.
	Foster a culture of trust and open communication.
	Encourage professional development and growth opportunities.
	Celebrate team and individual successes.
	Address conflicts and issues promptly and fairly.

Application in project management:

By nurturing your team and creating a positive work environment, you can enhance motivation, productivity and overall project success.

In the classic project world, 'team love' was about the gut instinct of the project manager or team leader; it was about cake or pizza, and it was definitely about a lot of coffee-fuelled check-ins. But in the world of the 'Invisible Project Manager', it will be a whole lot smarter, much subtler and just quietly systemised.

AI doesn't forget birthdays, it doesn't miss a drop in morale, and it doesn't wait until the retrospective to notice someone's disengaged.

Instead, it reads the 'room' digitally.

Here's how AI will probably cultivate team love:

- Understands motivation by constantly learning what drives each team member through behaviour, not guesswork.
- Delivers recognition through automatic identification of wins and through nudges of timely praise (never forgetting to say thank you).
- Builds trust by tracking team sentiment and collaboration health and giving early insights (without micromanaging – which none of us love).
- Supports growth by suggesting learning investments and proposing stretch opportunities tailored to each person's path and preferences.
- Celebrates success, anything from major milestones to teeny tiny triumphs (keeps the good vibes flowing).
- Prevents conflicts by spotting tension points early through tone and activity patterns, and by taking (or recommending) action before it all explodes (extreme case).

Team love in this AI-powered world isn't emotional guesswork, and it isn't dependent on human variability, or stress or lack of focus; it's just quiet intelligent care.

Soulless I hear you say. Maybe, but efficient, and there is always that 'human in the loop' escape route. But I do acknowledge that we do have to manage the mental health aspect in a good way in the new world.

Less effort with more impact.

Because when your team feels valued, supported and seen, the project doesn't just succeed – it thrives.

6.10 Controlled accessibility

Balance availability with productivity.

Access balance:

'Being there when you are really needed and being there all the time are very different things indeed.'[1718]

Managed availability. Balancing accessibility with productivity is crucial for effective project management. While being available to your team is important, constant interruptions can hinder productivity and decision-making.

Strategies for controlled accessibility:
- Establish clear communication channels and protocols.
- Set specific 'office hours' for open-door policy.
- Use delegation effectively to empower team members.
- Implement a system for prioritising requests and issues.
- Educate team members on when and how to escalate concerns.
- Regularly review and adjust your accessibility approach.

Application in project management:
By implementing controlled accessibility, project managers can maintain team support while preserving time for critical tasks and decision-making.

With AI platforms assuming pretty much the majority of communication, there will be a massive reduction in human-to-human interaction.

Which, in turn, will lead to the need for a critical rise in focus and speed of attention when the digital channels of communication escalate to the 'human in the loop' level.

All the above will still stand but for a small subset rather than for the common or majority of interactions. The result will be a rise in productivity as a result.

6.11 Project closure

Learn from the missing links.

Project closing:

'Lessons learned should be lessons shared, so don't be mean, share it out!'[19]

Knowledge capture and transfer. Proper project closure involves more than just delivering the final product. It's an opportunity to capture valuable insights, learn from experiences and improve future project performance.

Key steps in effective project closure:	Conduct a thorough project retrospective. Identify what you know, don't know and didn't know you didn't know. Document lessons learned and best practices. Share insights with team members and stakeholders. Incorporate learnings into future project planning and processes. Celebrate project achievements and team contributions.

Application in project management:

By dedicating time and effort to proper project closure, you can enhance organisational knowledge, improve future project performance and foster a culture of continuous learning and improvement.

I always say that at the end of the project you don't actually believe that you know everything that went on… no way!

And to be honest, even the AI project world won't know everything.

Project closure isn't about just ticking boxes; it's the moment we mine gold from the chaos (sorry, experience), and in the world of the 'Invisible Project Manager', AI will ensure those lessons aren't lost in forgotten folders or dusty retrospectives and weren't left behind just because 'there wasn't enough time'.

- Smart retrospectives: AI will track everything, all decisions, all delays, all mood shifts, all with the result that retrospectives no longer have to rely on memory (or guesswork).
  - It will analyse what went wrong, right and sideways by surfacing patterns and identifying surprises (minus the finger-pointing).
  - It will use auto-documentation as AI turns chat logs, tasks and meeting notes into clean, tagged and summarised lessons learned, all ripe and ready to share and use.
  - Insights will be pushed automatically into future projects, alerting teams before they repeat past mistakes, so we would really be in a world of lessons shared rather than lessons just talked about and put on a flipchart and stored behind someone's desk.
    - AI will prompt resulting recognition and wrap-up moments so that nobody's success or contribution slips through the cracks.

This really has to be a better world with actual project closure occurring even and every time.

6.12 And the conclusion

Yes.

The concept of productive laziness that I have been banging on about for the last 15 years (in books – longer in real life) does most certainly apply in this new age of artificial intelligence and the concept of the Fully Automated Project Manager (FAPM[20]) is spot on in applying that principle.

> *Lazy people are not idle or unproductive – they are just smart in the way they approach work.*
>
> (Peter Taylor, *The Lazy Project Manager,*[21] 2010)

CHATPBT

In the spirit of fairness (and laziness done well), let's look at how the timeless principles of *The Lazy Project Manager* hold up in the emerging world of AI-powered project management.

Smart Laziness, Meet Smart Machines. The 80/20 Rule still reigns supreme. Whether human or AI, success lies in focusing on the vital few:

- 20% of tasks drive 80% of results.
- 20% of stakeholders cause 80% of drama.
- 20% of use cases deliver 80% of business value.

AI doesn't rewrite the rule – it applies it ruthlessly. The Invisible Project Manager knows where to focus... and where not to.

Thick at the Ends, Thin in the Middle. Projects still look like dinosaurs: chunky upfront, lean in the middle, chunky at the end. AI supports both ends better – stronger setup, smoother closure – but the middle still runs on trust, empowerment and a well-oiled team.

Sponsor or Spectator? Sponsors are vital. Always have been. AI can support with insights and nudges, but you still need a human sponsor who knows their role. No excuses.

Project Creep: Handle with Lazy Discipline. Scope creep is human. AI won't forget the scope and won't add features just because someone asked nicely. That said, a strong change process still matters – for both AI and PMs.

Communicate Like You Mean It. Effective communication is still about what, when and how – only now with sentiment analysis, real-time translation and fewer 'lost in email' moments. AI reduces noise and boosts clarity. Win-win.

Fun, Team and a Bit of Cake. Can AI run pirate-themed retrospectives? Unlikely. But it can gamify tasks, track team morale and remind you to celebrate wins. It supports fun – but humans still spark it.

Crisis? Breathe First. AI spots trouble before it happens and stays calm when it does. Emotions don't cloud logic. So, less panic, more action.

Team Love, Digitally Delivered. AI doesn't forget birthdays or miss burnout signals. It watches, learns, nudges, praises and prevents conflict. That's not creepy – it's quietly caring. Welcome to automated empathy.

Always Available? No thanks. You don't need to be always on – just on when it matters. AI filters the noise and escalates what's important. That's controlled accessibility for the modern PM.

Closure: Not Just a Nice-to-Have. Project closure often gets skipped. Not anymore. AI tracks, documents, analyses and even nudges you to wrap things up right. Lessons learned become lessons shared – and actually reused.

Final Word. The Lazy Project Manager was always about working smarter. Now, with AI, that laziness is even lazier.

Notes

1 The concept of 'productive laziness' originates from Peter Taylor's book, *The Lazy Project Manager*, suggesting that by focusing on the most important tasks and eliminating unnecessary work, individuals can achieve greater efficiency and productivity.

2 The idea of 'productive laziness' also finds its roots in the Japanese concept of 'ma', which emphasises the importance of pauses and intervals, as well as perhaps the better-known Pareto Principle, which suggests that 80% of results come from 20% of efforts. This concept, sometimes called 'strategic laziness', advocates for prioritising high-impact tasks and minimising unnecessary effort to achieve greater productivity with less stress.

3 Quote from *The Lazy Project Manager* by Peter Taylor.

4 Extract from *The Lazy Project Manager* and *The Lazy Winning Project Manager* by Peter Taylor (Routledge).

5 The Pareto Principle, also known as the 80/20 rule, suggests that roughly 80% of effects come from 20% of causes. This principle can be applied to various

aspects of life and work, including time management, productivity and business strategy.

6 An algorithm is a well-defined, step-by-step procedure for solving a problem or completing a task that involves a sequence of operations that can be executed by a computer or a person.

7 Extract from *The Lazy Project Manager* and *The Lazy Winning Project Manager* by Peter Taylor (Routledge).

8 Extract from *The Lazy Project Manager* and *The Lazy Winning Project Manager* by Peter Taylor (Routledge).

9 Extract from *The Lazy Project Manager* and *The Lazy Winning Project Manager* by Peter Taylor (Routledge).

10 The Creep'o'Meter is a conceptual gauge or scale proposed by Peter Taylor that measures the degree of scope creep – the gradual expansion of a project's goals or deliverables beyond the originally agreed-upon scope, often without proper change control.

11 Extract from *The Lazy Project Manager* and *The Lazy Winning Project Manager* by Peter Taylor (Routledge).

12 Extract from *The Lazy Project Manager* and *The Lazy Winning Project Manager* by Peter Taylor (Routledge).

13 This is not a joke; it is a real 'International Day' – http://www.talklikeapirate.com/piratehome.html – have fun 'talking' like a pirate, using email 'translators' to create pirate speech communication, and even slap on an eye patch and a parrot to get into the mood. Just for the one day you understand, any more than that and you are probably just odd.

14 Some people are more creative due to a combination of inherent traits, nurtured abilities and cultivated practices, including openness to experience, curiosity, passion, flexibility and a willingness to embrace new ideas and perspectives. While genetics play a minor role (around 22%), the majority of creative performance is influenced by environmental factors and learned behaviours – together with the freedom to be so creative.

15 Extract from *The Lazy Project Manager* and *The Lazy Winning Project Manager* by Peter Taylor (Routledge).

16 Extract from *The Lazy Project Manager* and *The Lazy Winning Project Manager* by Peter Taylor (Routledge).

17 Mental health refers to our emotional, psychological and social well-being. It influences how we think, feel and act, and it impacts how we handle stress, interact with others and make choices. Good mental health is essential for overall well-being, enabling individuals to realise their potential, cope with life's challenges and contribute to their teams and communities.

18 Extract from *The Lazy Project Manager* and *The Lazy Winning Project Manager* by Peter Taylor (Routledge).

19 Extract from *The Lazy Project Manager* and *The Lazy Winning Project Manager* by Peter Taylor (Routledge).

20 OK, I am fully aware that there is another 'FAPM' acronym in the project world already, the FAPM (Fellows of APM). Now it is not explicitly stated, but it is implied that there are a few thousand of such folks. APM (Association for Project Management) has over 40,000 members, and FAPM is an exclusive membership level for those who have demonstrated expertise and made significant contributions to the project profession. While all members of APM are part of a large community, only a select few achieve the FAPM status, signifying a high level of achievement and contribution. But I am sorry, the term

FAPM will take over very soon in describing the autonomous project world and so APM might do well to either a) protect the acronym (if that is possible) or b) find a new one for their members.

21 *The Lazy Project Manager: How to Be Twice as Productive and Still Leave the Office Early* (Infinite Ideas Ltd, 2010) Author: Peter Taylor.

Chapter 7

A professional objective comparison

7.1 Only being (objectively) fair

So moving on from a direct comparison with my own body of work[1] let us now consider an 'industry standard' from the biggest project association with their 'body of knowledge.[2]

The Project Management Body of Knowledge (PMBOK) Guide, created by the Project Management Institute (PMI), has evolved significantly since its inception in 1987. Initially published as a white paper, it has been updated through several editions, with each reflecting changes and advancements in project management practices and standards. The PMBOK Guide serves as a foundational resource for all project managers and is essential reading for all those preparing for the PMP[3] exam.

The 7th edition[4] shifts the focus from a process-based approach to a principles-based approach which emphasises value delivery and outcomes over strict deliverables. It introduces 12 project management principles and 8 performance domains to guide project managers in delivering successful project outcomes, and it also emphasises tailoring project management approaches to the specific context of each unique project.

Key changes and focus:

- Principles-based approach: Instead of focusing solely on processes, highlighting 12 guiding principles for project management.
- Value delivery: The guide emphasises the importance of delivering value to stakeholders and the organisation.
- Outcomes-focused: The emphasis is on achieving desired outcomes rather than just completing specific tasks.
- Performance domains: Eight performance domains are introduced, providing a framework for managing different aspects of a project.
- Tailoring: The guide encourages project managers to adapt their approach based on the unique context of each project.

DOI: 10.4324/9781003672357-7

OK, good stuff of course, but how does that compare with, say, AI today?

What are the aspects that an AI-powered project world could handle, and in all fairness, what can it not handle?

Now, once again, I am not claiming to be able to see into the future and I am also not claiming to be an expert in AI (just an enthusiast), but the following statements of the 'As-Is' and the prediction of the 'To-Be' are wholly realistic in my personal view.

But, of course, it is a personal view and you are totally free to disagree.

7.2 Project management principles (12 principles)

These are broad, behaviour-based guidelines for effective project management.

Table 7.1 Project management principles

Principle	*AI potential*	*Commentary*
Stewardship	Not Replaceable	Ethical and responsible management requires human judgment.
Team	Not Replaceable	Building and nurturing teams is a human-intensive activity.
Stakeholders	Assist	AI can analyse stakeholders but not build trust or negotiate.
Value	Assist	AI can track and analyse value delivery, but decisions require context.
Systems Thinking	Assist	AI can model systems but not fully grasp organisational dynamics.
Leadership	Not Replaceable	Inspiring and guiding people remains a human strength.
Tailoring	Assist	AI can recommend frameworks based on context, but tailoring is nuanced.
Quality	Replace/Assist	AI can monitor quality metrics and flag issues, even take corrective actions.
Complexity	Assist	AI excels at analysing complexity but lacks intuitive insight.
Risk	Replace/Assist	AI is highly capable of predictive analytics and scenario modelling.
Adaptability	Assist	AI can suggest adaptive strategies based on patterns.
Change	Assist	AI can recommend and track change initiatives, but human buy-in is key.

7.3 Performance domains (8 domains)

These are areas of focus that contribute to the successful delivery of project outcomes.

Table 7.2 Performance domains

Domain	*AI potential*	*Commentary*
Stakeholder	Assist	AI can identify and monitor stakeholders but not manage relationships.
Team	Not Replaceable	Team dynamics and motivation require emotional intelligence.
Development Approach and Lifecycle	Replace/Assist	AI can recommend approaches and automate lifecycle stages.
Lifecycle Planning	Replace/Assist	AI can generate plans, forecasts and schedules based on input data.
Project Work	Replace/Assist	AI can automate reporting, monitoring and some coordination.
Delivery	Assist	AI can monitor delivery progress, but human intervention needed to ensure value alignment.
Measurement	Replaceable	AI is strong in KPIs, dashboards and real-time analytics.
Uncertainty	Assist	AI is powerful in scenario planning, simulations and forecasting.

7.4 Tailoring

Tailoring refers to adapting processes, tools and methodologies to fit the context.

AI Role: Assist

AI can suggest tailoring options based on similar past projects or organisational data, but final decisions depend on culture, people and strategic direction.

7.5 Models, methods and artefacts

These include:

- Models: Such as, communication models, motivation models.
- Methods: Such as, critical path, lean, backlog refinement.
- Artefacts: Such as, business case, schedule, risk register

Table 7.3 Models, methods and artefacts

Element	*AI potential*	*Commentary*
Models	Replace/Assist	AI can apply and even refine models using machine learning.
Methods	Replace/Assist	Many methods can be automated or recommended by AI.
Artefacts	Replaceable	Documentation and templates can be auto generated and managed by AI.

A mix of replace and/or assist in these three elements.

7.6 System for value delivery

This overarching concept emphasises delivering outcomes that provide value to stakeholders.

AI Role: Assist
While AI can monitor and report value-related metrics, understanding strategic impact and long-term value creation is still a human role.

While AI can assist or even replace many technical and data-driven tasks, areas involving leadership, ethics, empathy and stakeholder engagement still require a human touch. The future of project management is human + AI collaboration, not replacement.

7.7 That is now, what about in 10 years

So even today the coverage of AI is quite significant, but what about in, say, 10 years from now? To get our heads around this, we do need to look ahead in time and consider the speed and growth of AI next year, in five years, in ten years.

The following is an assumptive projection based on the speed and capability of artificial progress that is (more than) likely to occur over the next few years. I am picking ten years, but I am quietly confident that it will happen in 5 years or less, so 2030.

7.8 The 12 principles – 2035

These are broad, behaviour-based guidelines for effective project management.

Table 7.4 The 10-year view for effective project management

Principle	*AI potential*	*Commentary*
Stewardship	Assist	Ethics, trust and accountability will likely still require human oversight.
Team	Assist	Even with AI emotional modelling, building genuine human rapport remains difficult.
Stakeholders	Replaceable	AI could handle communication, negotiation, sentiment analysis and influence strategies.
Value	Replaceable	AI could understand and optimise for multi-dimensional stakeholder value across time.
Systems Thinking	Replaceable	AI can model dynamic systems far better than humans and propose holistic strategies.
Leadership	Not Replaceable	Human charisma, cultural nuance and ethical vision will still be uniquely human.
Tailoring	Replaceable	AI will likely self-adjust methodologies based on real-time context across industries.
Quality	Replaceable	Fully autonomous quality management with predictive corrections is highly likely.
Complexity	Replaceable	AI will thrive in complexity modelling and adaptive response planning.
Risk	Replaceable	Risk anticipation and mitigation will be AI-dominated.
Adaptability	Replaceable	AI systems will autonomously evolve strategies and plans as conditions change.
Change	Assist	Driving behavioural change still hinges on human influence, despite AI modelling change impact.

If you compare the now assessment to the 10-year view you will see that 8 out of the 12 principles have moved into the AI domain.

Three principles remain as 'assist' by AI, but I would argue here that much of these three principles would be undertaken effectively by AI with only a very small 'human in the loop' intervention.

As such only one, that is leadership, remains truly outside the AI management scope.

7.9 The eight domains – 2035

These are areas of focus that contribute to the successful delivery of project outcomes.

Seven out of the eight domains progress into the AI-powered world, with one already identified as replaceable even today.

Table 7.5 The 10-year view for Performance domains

Domain	*AI potential*	*Commentary*
Stakeholder	Replaceable	AI will manage, predict and influence stakeholders using behavioural models and NLP.
Team	Assist Only	People leadership still depends on trust and empathy but AI can support while not lead humans.
Development Approach and Lifecycle	Replaceable	AI will select, tailor and automate lifecycle management in real time.
Lifecycle Planning	Replaceable	AI will produce optimal, self-correcting plans dynamically.
Project Work	Replaceable	Project execution oversight and status management will be AI-driven.
Delivery	Replaceable	AI will ensure continuous delivery and feedback loops.
Measurement	Replaceable	Fully automated analytics and performance tracking will dominate.
Uncertainty	Replaceable	AI will simulate complex futures and recommend proactive strategies.

7.10 Tailoring – 2035

Tailoring refers to adapting processes, tools and methodologies to fit the context.

Status: Replaceable
Rationale: AI will learn from millions of contextual projects and dynamically adapt frameworks better than humans ever could.

7.11 Models, methods and artefacts – 2035

These include:

- Models: Such as, communication models, motivation models.
- Methods: Such as, critical path, lean, backlog refinement.
- Artefacts: Such as, business case, schedule, risk register

Progression to fully replaceable by AI is the clear expectation here, absolute progression from the 'now' state.

Table 7.6 The 10-year view of models, methods and artefacts

Element	*AI potential*	*Commentary*
Models	Replaceable	AI will generate, evolve and apply models automatically.
Methods	Replaceable	AI will execute and modify methods in real time, based on outcomes.
Artefacts	Replaceable	Autonomous generation, analysis and versioning will be standard.

7.12 System for value delivery – 2035

This overarching concept emphasises delivering outcomes that provide value to stakeholders.

Status: Replaceable
Rationale: AI will be capable of simulating and optimising for long-term stakeholder value, adjusting strategies based on evolving data.

7.13 The PMBOK 8th edition is coming

Ah, the PMBOK Guide, beloved by some, feared by many and frequently used as an improvised doorstop by the rest of us, has an 8th edition just around the corner (Q3 2025 apparently).

Here's what's changing:

- The 8th edition reintroduces 40 processes nestled comfortably into the good old 5 process groups from the 6th edition and wrapped in 7 performance domains.
- PMI has trimmed down its guiding principles from 12 to 6.
- Down from eight to seven are the domains, but this time they're process-driven and focused on the essentials: Governance, Scope, Schedule, Finance, Stakeholders, Quality and Resources.
- There's a shiny new appendix on Artificial Intelligence (I guess because pretending AI isn't part of project life now is like pretending Excel will ever go away – I hope it does, one day).
- The new guide embraces hybrid thinking (finally) because real-world projects are messy.

The intention being that for those just entering the PM world, this is a more usable, more grounded guide.

7.14 The PMBOK 10th edition

I imagine by the time my conceptual 10-year horizon has arrived, PMI will be banging out its 10th edition, but will it matter by then? I mean, how can they (or any of the associations) keep pace with the speed of change that is coming!

See my 'big questions' later on, in this book.

7.15 The 10-year AI replacement

So where does that leave us all? Well, pretty much where I am predicting we will be:

- Principles (12) – Mostly replaceable.
- Performance Domains (8) – Mostly replaceable.
- Tailoring – Replaceable.
- Models, Methods, and Artefacts – Fully replaceable.
- System for Value Delivery – Replaceable.

In 10 years:

- AI could run 80–90% of project management functions autonomously (FAPM).
- The human project management role will evolve into strategic stewardship, ethical oversight and cultural leadership responsibilities.
- This validates my concept of *The Invisible Project Manager* where projects will still happen, but the visible manager is now AI.

CHATPBT

Let's take a pause from comparing everything to the author's brilliant work (tempting though that is) and be fair – objectively fair – and look at the PMBOK® Guide, that ever-evolving, ever-expanding juggernaut of project management wisdom.

The 7th edition made quite the leap – from the comfort of process checklists to the brave new world of principles, performance domains and tailoring. All good stuff: Value over volume, outcomes over outputs and flexibility over formula. But let's ask the awkward question – what of AI?

Today, AI can assist with tailoring, support value tracking and even replace a good chunk of the methods and artefacts toolbox. Fast-forward ten years (or five, let's be honest), and the AI story gets bolder. Most of those 12 principles? AI-owned. Performance domains? Tick. Tailoring? Replaced. Methods and models? History. Value systems? Simulated and optimised by machines.

Even PMI is catching up, with the 8th edition now dragging AI into the spotlight and bringing back some old favourites to keep traditionalists happy. But let's not kid ourselves – by the 10th edition, we may be applauding an AI co-author or just not bother making that edition.

Which brings us full circle to The Invisible Project Manager: Still delivering value, but now largely unseen – and probably silicon-based.

Notes

1 Random fact: The Lazy Project Manager's initial working title was 'The Lazy Body of Knowledge', but even I felt, at that time in my career as a speaker/author, this was a bit too confrontational.

2 Yes, there are other models and frameworks and bodies of knowledge, but I don't want to bore you, reader, with too many comparisons. I am sure you get the general idea.

3 Project Management Professional (PMP) is an internationally recognised professional designation offered by the Project Management Institute (PMI).

4 The go-to source for Project Managers, the PMBOK® Guide (7th edition) is structured around eight Project Management domains and identifies twelve key principles of Project Management. This latest edition reflects the ever-evolving nature of Project Management approaches due to emerging technologies and rapid market changes. Publisher Project Management Institute – Publication Date – August 2021.

Chapter 8

The myth of irreplaceability

8.1 Pushback is inevitable

They used to joke that change was inevitable, except from a vending machine, but these days even that is no longer true with mobile payment on vending machines solving the whole change issue.

> Intelligence is what we learn. Wisdom is what we unlearn.
>
> (J.R. Rim)

There will, of course, be an emotional pushback.

This is guaranteed, isn't it? I mean it is not merely an observation; it will happen with the rise of automation, with the rise of artificial intelligence, and with the kind of algorithmic governance that spreads across every domain of work.

Project management stands at a pivotal crossroads (hence the, hopefully, timely writing of this book).

Project management carries a very unique cultural weight since it is often perceived not just as a function, but as a form of leadership. You know, we all talk in the industry about the science of project management and the art of project management as a form of extra validation perhaps or in a way to explore how complicated it all is and how valued we should all be.

Therefore, when we talk about removing or replacing that function with automation, the coldness of automation, we're not just talking about a shifting process; what we are actually talking about is a shift in actual identity. So, if you think about the fallacy of project management exceptionalism, this really is a belief that our domain, our world, is somehow completely immune to automation. The projects, with their ambiguity, projects with their complexity and projects with all of the human variables that require human steering are beyond the capability of automation.

DOI: 10.4324/9781003672357-8

To be fair, this fallacy emerges from a place of pride, I guess, but also probably from fear; pride in the belief that only we can manage this chaos, this is our DNA,[1] this is our world, and fear is that we will no longer be needed. Then, if this is the case, what on earth are we going to do?

This fallacy has persisted for many decades, and project managers are often seen as the kind of glue holding everything together, navigating changing and shifting requirements, and dealing with difficult and complex stakeholders, leading and inspiring very fragile team members and team dynamics. And for a long time that perception was very valid, but I don't think it is any longer a reflection of the current or the future realities.

This is the challenge of the change that we're going through.

Modern AI systems can already digest enormous volumes of data; we've seen that they can 'learn' at unbelievable speeds from historical project performance. They can generate real-time risk forecasts and optimise resource allocations or flag scope creep delivery threats way faster than any human, and more consistently than any human, as long as it's got the data to feed on, of course. In other words, the science of project management has matured to the point that it can be and will be increasingly automated, and yet still, the idea of a project manager being replaced is almost sacrilegious. Of course, when it's your own profession that is being challenged, well, of course you're going to get very defensive, because we conflate leadership with management; we think that if no one is in charge, then the project will spiral into chaos. Failure is the only possible outcome.

I challenge this, and I suggest that this is becoming an outdated idea.

8.2 The psychological comfort of being in charge

Part of the resistance to automation in project management, I think, stems from this very human need for reassurance; stakeholders like knowing that someone is there on the end of the phone line, at the other side of an email, even down the end of the corridor in the office, for people who still work in an office. They can call on them and someone would then take responsibility, someone who could be blamed, or someone who could be praised.

This is a psychological anchor in a play if you like, as humans are comforted by hierarchies and by authoritative figures. They believe projects are just safer when someone is just watching out, even if that person isn't necessarily steering more effectively than, say, an algorithm would. This belief system, the comfort of command, is totally hardwired into almost every organisation. It's reflected in our organisation with charts, in our job descriptions, and in our performance reviews. We don't just assign work, we assign ownership, and we like knowing that someone is on the hook at all times.

Therefore, removing the human Project Manager challenges this norm. It causes consternation when a digital system is in control, when systems self-adjust and update and respond and manage and prioritisation is handled autonomously. Then people start asking, well hang on, who is actually accountable?

They stop asking, who's managing the people, and they ask who's leading this. This discomfort is natural, but I believe it's also temporary.

I was in Los Angeles back in 2024 and was intrigued to see the Waymo[2] taxis roaming the streets. It was a very alien sight. But to be fair, they weren't 'roaming'; they were effectively and safely navigating the streets and providing a service to people wanting to get around. Sadly, I could not access these vehicles (you had to have pre-registered, and tests were limiting the number of passengers) as I would have loved to have a go, but I was convinced that this is, indeed, the future of taxi services.[3] We will very rapidly come to accept this as a norm.

8.3 A case for letting go

Relax, there will be no singing the song from Frozen (although I did get one project conference of 400 people sing along to this one – it is out there on the web somewhere).

The future of project delivery will not require someone in charge.

It will require someone in support, a facilitator, a steward of value, maybe not even that.

But to get there we need to let go, not because project managers are no longer important but because the traditional form of a project no longer does the job at the speed, the scale or the complexity of modern project demands.

It's incredibly fortunate that artificial intelligence is arriving at a level of maturity at precisely the right time, because we were already struggling to deal with the extended capabilities and demands and complexities of the projects across the world today.

Now, letting go doesn't automatically mean chaos. It means trusting in data and system design and automation that is faster, that is more accurate and it is more consistent than any human could ever be. It means shifting from control over to a world of orchestration, from command to a world of enablement.

I'll be honest, this shift is going to be hard. I certainly don't underestimate the effort that is going to be required to make this transformation just as I realise that for many, being a project manager is not just simply a role, it's a source of identity. Titles like programme director or PMO leader carry weight inside organisations, and this is something that's evolved over a long period of time. Throughout my career, I've seen the respect grow for project managers, project leaders, programme directors and all the rest, and it therefore represents years of experience, years of hard-earned respect and significant strategic involvement in many cases, but, you know, clinging to the illusion of indispensability is only going to delay the inevitable transformation.

Resistance is futile.[4]

8.4 A matter of trust

One of the really big barriers to AI assuming the majority of any work, let alone project management, is the aspect of trust.

Trust is the confident belief in the reliability, integrity and competence of a person or system. It means feeling secure that someone will act honestly, keep their commitments, and act in your best interests, even when you are not watching.

The Edelman Trust Barometer 2025[5] tells us something rather interesting, or perhaps rather worrying depending on your perspective. Apparently, while 76% of us trust 'technology', only 50% of us trust 'AI'. Now that's a 26-point gap or enough space to park a fleet of self-driving Teslas[6] and still squeeze in a drone or two.

The report[7] goes on

> AI trust is divided. In China, 72% of people express trust in AI. In the U.S., that number drops to 32%. This isn't just a difference in policy or regulation it's a reflection of how societies perceive risk, control, and opportunity. Some see AI as a force for progress, while others worry about its unintended consequences. Trust disparities don't stop at national borders. Older adults, those with a lower-income, and women are less likely to trust AI. This signals an opportunity: AI leaders who address these concerns directly through inclusion, transparency, and demonstrated benefits will be the ones who build durable trust.

But hold on, aren't AI and technology just the same thing?

First off, yes, people still love their tech (I do, and you do and seems like everyone does), we trust our phones to wake us up (true with the single exception of when I have to get up for an early flight when I stress that today will be the day that the phone won't ring the alarm!). We trust our GPS to get us to work, and we even trust our hyper-sophisticated coffee machines (most days). But with artificial intelligence, it may seem to be a different story.

You see, AI isn't just helpful anymore; it's everywhere, and it's just doing stuff for us. And while we use it daily, we're not entirely sure it's got our very best interests at heart. I guess it is a bit like trusting a clever colleague who never blinks and seemingly knows everything.

Now this apparent trust gap could have significant consequences because if half the population doesn't trust AI, then how do we expect them to embrace autonomous cars, AI doctors or autonomous project managers (now there's a scary thought)? General hesitation might slow progress (especially if the most senior business leaders lack understanding or react with fear, uncertainty and doubt).

But let's not panic just yet.

What does 'trust' even mean in this context?

Do people trust AI to do a job well?

- To be fair.
- To be reasonable.
- To not go rogue and start a robot uprising Terminator[8] style.

That's a lot of ground to cover in one word. And let's be honest: Most people already use AI without knowing it, from Netflix[9] recommendations to spellcheck, from Amazon interactions to navigational guidance. If they're already using it, maybe the trust gap is more about perception than reality.

Well, whether the gap is real or imagined, big or exaggerated, it matters, because how we feel about AI will shape how it's rolled out, regulated and received. If trust is low, then organisations will need to work very hard to earn it with transparency, ethics and maybe a lot more openness.

The Edelman Trust Barometer 2025 continues with some sage advice about progressing to a state of trust.

> AI isn't just about efficiency it's about impact. Only 44% of people globally feel comfortable with businesses using AI, and in the U.S., that number is even lower. This presents a clear challenge: organizations that fail to address trust concerns will face resistance. The ones that prioritize transparency, fairness, and clear use cases will be best positioned to build long-term trust and drive meaningful adoption and seize competitive advantage.

A playbook approach is proposed:

> Earning trust isn't a one-time initiative it's an ongoing commitment. Companies leading in AI adoption should focus on:
>
> - Transparency First: Explain how AI works, what it does, and who benefits.
> - Proactive Governance: Getting ahead of regulation ensures AI is safe, fair, and accountable.

- Demonstrated Impact: Real-world applications that improve lives will drive acceptance and trust.
- Engaging the Public: Listening, responding, and including diverse voices in AI's evolution will strengthen confidence.

This interesting report (I do suggest that you check it out yourself) concludes with a voice of optimism and selective opportunity:

> The opportunity is clear: AI can be a force for progress, efficiency, and inclusion. But it will take deliberate action to ensure that people trust its potential as much as they believe in its power. The future may include AI reshaping the workforce, but the industry must do a better job of illustrating what that means new industries emerging, jobs evolving, and productivity gains fuelling economic growth. AI is not just about automation; it's about augmentation, unlocking human potential in ways we have yet to fully realize. The companies that get this right will shape the next era of innovation and prosperity.

Some more thoughts from a collection of wise people.

> The key question is: can we trust AI to do what we expect – and only what we expect?
>
> Fei-Fei Li[10]

> The challenge is not whether AI can make decisions, but whether humans can trust those decisions – and understand them.
>
> (Tim O'Reilly)[11]

> Trust in AI is earned, not given. It's built through transparency, consistency, and understanding.
>
> (Francesca Rossi)[12]

> Humans won't trust what they don't understand. And they shouldn't.
>
> (Cynthia Rudin)[13]

> Technology doesn't replace people. It augments their capacity to lead, decide, and create.
>
> (Andrew Ng)[14]

> We should be more willing [to hand over judgments] because in many situations it's been established scientifically that algorithms and even very simple rules perform better than humans.
>
> (Daniel Kahneman)[15]

> Machines will do what they are told. The danger is that we might not always tell them the right thing.
>
> (Nick Bostrom)[16]

As we move inevitably towards the era of the 'Invisible Project Manager', the narrative of automation and efficiency covers a very tricky aspect: That of ethics. When a human project manager decides something, no matter if that decision is inspired or fundamentally flawed, they are, by default, accountable. But when AI makes a decision in the future, then who is responsible?

In an age where AI runs projects autonomously, who signs off the risk register, or who approves a milestone or a stage gate, and who is liable when things go off the rails? These aren't theoretical concerns at all; they boardroom, legal and societal concerns.

Governments and institutions are already waking up to AI's impact, for example, the EU AI Act[17] classifies project management AI under 'high-risk' use cases if it impacts human welfare, employment or safety (not all projects are equal, are they?).

We will see in the future,

- Certification requirements for enterprise-grade AI PMs.
- Audit mandates to track decisions.
- Liability frameworks for errors and damages.
- Industry codes of conduct for ethical automation.

Until then, forward-thinking PMOs must self-regulate by,

- Use AI ethically by design.
- Document AI governance procedures.
- Define escalation paths when AI behaviour is uncertain and when the 'human in the loop' is essential.

Personally, I just believe trust will come with use, with time. Just think about how rapidly you trusted your handheld devices, Google and now ChatGPT etc., and navigation through Waze; all those apps you love in your modern life.

It's a kind of proof of the pudding[18] situation, isn't it.

8.5 Project science versus project art

Back to project management now. Perhaps the most persistent argument against automation will be that project management is as much an art as it is a science. And this is true, but only in part.

Yes, there is art in leadership, there is a nuance in stakeholder development, there is emotional intelligence required when guiding people through change, but the operational backbone of projects, the scheduling, the risk management, cost tracking, the reporting, the dependency mapping, etc. well it's pure science. And science, by its very nature, is repeatable, it is measurable, it is automatable.[19] The challenge though is that many project managers feel they have spent their careers doing the science while calling it art. What feels like gut instinct is often actually pattern recognition, what feels like improvisation is often actually just actual experience which is manifesting predictability.

These two can therefore both be encoded; they can be modelled, they can be automated. Project art, if you like, the leadership, the empathy, the communication skills can still be preserved, but it no longer needs to sit within the boundaries of traditional project management roles. Instead, it will emerge through product owners, through team coaches, AI trainers, and even through the interfaces users use to interact with their digital project systems. And this is really important. What we must accept is that the art will also be taken over, and it's not because we as project managers, as project professionals, have failed; oh no, it is because we have succeeded in codifying best practices so exceptionally that machines could now and will now execute them just as well, and probably even better.

8.6 The path forward

In order to move into this next era of project delivery, what we must do is unlearn as much as we have learned.

> The illiterate of the future are not those who can't read or write but those who cannot learn, unlearn, and relearn.
>
> (Alvin Toffler)[20]

We must unlearn the belief that control equals safety and unlearn the idea that a single human must always be accountable, and we must unlearn the myth that project management is somehow uniquely human.

Instead, what we must do is embrace systems that make decisions in real time; we must reimagine PMOs (my world) as centres of value, focused not on process but on outcome. We must train our project teams to interpret, refine and interact with 'project intelligence systems'.

I can reflect at this point on a piece of thought leadership I put down back in 2018 on this very subject (what follows is an extract from that piece):

Project Intelligence (PI) refers to the skills, processes, technologies, applications, metrics and practices used to support successful project delivery from the organisation as a whole.

Common components of Project Intelligence include:

- *Project Management skills, maturity and certification (from project contributor through to senior project (or program) roles).*
- *Project methodologies and practices.*
- *Project Management Information Systems.*
- *Project (or Program) Management Office (PMO) activities and focus (supportive, directive, controlling).*
- *Executive/Management skills, maturity and experience in project delivery.*
- *Project-based organisational maturity.*
- *Project Support technologies (Resource Management, Skills Database, Scheduling and Time Management, Invoicing or Cost Management).*
- *Project Dashboard and Reporting technologies.*

Project Intelligence aims to support a project-based organisations successful project capability.

Now way back in 2018 I had no thoughts along artificial intelligence, even though virtual assistants and chatbots were becoming more common. That said, it seems to me that I was already moving slowly along a path that would eventually and progressively move towards the AI empowered project manager, and that, in turn, would lead naturally on to the thoughts around the 'Invisible Project Manager'. But I am sure most people haven't considered this endgame possibility and, as such, the emotional pushback will definitely come.

Some will resist, perhaps many will resist, and others will I think, try to carve out a new human-only domain (Luddites?[21] Time will tell). But over time, outcomes will speak louder than tradition, and when all the dust settles, when we have progressed through the next few years, we will realise something incredibly powerful. We will realise that letting go of the old model does not diminish our own value or that of our profession. Instead, it will amplify it, because in the space where task management used to live, new leadership can emerge, leadership grounded not in checklists and tick boxes and all the rest of it, but leadership grounded in vision, not in authority, but in impact. And I believe that is the true art of modern project delivery.

In the words of Ozzy Osbourne[22] 'We are going through changes' and we certainly are.

CHATPBT

Let's get one thing straight from the start: The robots are not just coming – they're already here, and they've got a Gantt Chart, a risk matrix and they've already optimised your schedule before your first coffee. And yes, naturally, that's freaking a lot of people out.

You see, project management isn't just a job – it's a culture, a belief system, a lifestyle, a deeply emotional security blanket for many. PMs have long been seen as the glue, the guides, the grown-ups in the room. We don't just manage timelines – we lead! We inspire! We fight dragons in stakeholder meetings!

So when we say automation and AI can now do most of that science-y stuff – scheduling, risk, budgeting, resourcing – better, faster and without asking for annual leave... well, understandably, people clutch their PRINCE2 certificates a little tighter.

But let's be honest: The belief that project management is magically immune to automation is less fact, more fairy tale. We tell ourselves we're too emotionally intelligent, too nuanced, too irreplaceable. But guess what? Machines are learning fast, and they don't even need coffee breaks.

Still, the discomfort is real. The idea of letting go feels like professional treason. Like someone's asking us to sing Let It Go at a project conference. (Oh wait, Peter actually did that...)

But letting go doesn't mean chaos – it means trust. It means we shift from control freaks to value stewards. From micromanagers to mission enablers. From PMs to... whatever comes next. (Maybe Chief Outcome Whisperers?)

Trust, by the way, is a sticky issue. According to the Edelman Trust Barometer, people love 'technology' but get nervous when you call it 'AI.' It's like saying 'I like dogs' but locking up your Roomba because it's too clever. Why? Because AI doesn't just do stuff – it decides stuff. And when something makes decisions without a warm smile or a LinkedIn profile, we get twitchy.

So yes, we need to unlearn a few things. Like the idea that only a human can manage change. Or that emotional intelligence is immune to modelling. Or that only real leaders can wear lanyards. Because here's the kicker: We've done our jobs so well – we've made ourselves automatable.

So the next time someone says, 'the machines are taking over', just smile and say, 'Good. I've got bigger things to do.'

As Ozzy wisely put it: 'We're going through changes.'

And we are.

Notes

1 DNA stands for Deoxyribonucleic Acid. It's the molecule that carries the genetic instructions used in the growth, development, functioning and reproduction of all living organisms and many viruses.

2 Waymo is an American autonomous driving technology company and a subsidiary of Alphabet Inc., the parent company of Google. It was launched in 2009 as the Google Self-Driving Car Project and later rebranded as Waymo in 2016.

3 Tesla's concept of Cybercabs envisions a fleet of fully electric, self-driving vehicles operating as autonomous taxis, providing on-demand, shared transportation services powered by Tesla's Full Self-Driving technology. The aim would be to reduce the need for private car ownership, lower transportation costs and decrease emissions by combining electric vehicle efficiency with advanced AI-driven autonomy, ultimately transforming urban mobility into a more convenient, affordable and sustainable experience.

4 The phrase 'Resistance is futile' is most famously associated with the Borg, a fictional alien collective from the Star Trek universe. While Douglas Adams, author of The Hitchhiker's Guide to the Galaxy, didn't coin 'Resistance is futile', he did explore similarly absurd and ironic themes about technological inevitability, bureaucracy and the futility of human effort in the face of a chaotic universe.

5 The Edelman Trust Barometer 2025 – The barometer offers annual global reports on the data gathered through surveys conducted in nearly 30 countries. The surveys include questions on the population's trust in media (including search engines, social media, owned media and traditional media), the government and/or societal leaders, NGOs and businesses.

6 Tesla cars are a range of all-electric vehicles produced by Tesla, Inc. These vehicles are known for their electric powertrains, sleek designs and advanced technology features, including over-the-air software updates. Other electric vehicles are, of course, available.

7 https://www.edelman.com/trust/2025/trust-barometer/report-tech-sector

8 The Terminator is a 1984 American science fiction action film directed by James Cameron starring Arnold Schwarzenegger as the Terminator, a cybernetic assassin sent back in time from 2029 to 1984 to assassinate Sarah Connor whose unborn son will one day save mankind from extinction by Skynet, a hostile artificial intelligence, in a post-apocalyptic future. Probably the most used imagery when it comes to talking about AI.

9 Netflix is a subscription-based streaming service that provides access to a wide variety of TV shows, movies, anime, documentaries and more, available on internet-connected devices.

10 Fei-Fei Li is a Chinese American computer scientist renowned for her pioneering work in artificial intelligence (AI), particularly in computer vision. https://issues.org/interview-godmother-ai-fei-fei-li/

11 Tim O'Reilly is a well-known technology publisher, author and entrepreneur who has played a significant role in shaping the modern tech landscape.

12 Francesca Rossi is an Italian computer scientist renowned for her pioneering work in artificial intelligence (AI), particularly in AI ethics, constraint reasoning and preference modelling.

13 Cynthia Rudin is a leading American computer scientist and statistician specialising in interpretable machine learning.

14 Andrew Ng is a globally recognised leader in artificial intelligence (AI), renowned for his contributions to both AI research and education. He is the founder and CEO of Landing AI, founder of DeepLearning.AI, co-founder and executive chairman of Coursera. https://www.businessinsider.com/andrew-ng-ai-jobs-workers-optimist-economy-2024-7?utm_source=chatgpt.com
15 Daniel Kahneman is a renowned psychologist and economist, best known for his groundbreaking work on human judgement, decision-making and behavioural economics. https://www.contagious.com/iq/article/daniel-kahneman-and-olivier-sibony-on-the-blind-spots-of-judgement?utm_source=chatgpt.com
16 Nick Bostrom is a Swedish philosopher and leading thinker on the future of humanity, artificial intelligence and existential risks. https://www.reddit.com/r/Futurology/comments/341mzo/nick_bostrom_what_happens_when_our_computers_get/?rdt=55204
17 The European Union's AI Act represents a landmark effort to regulate AI, balancing innovation with ethical considerations. The AI Act seeks to keep AI safe by establishing a comprehensive legal framework ensuring that these technologies are developed and used in a transparent manner that is aligned with fundamental rights. Under the AI Act, any organisation using AI tools to assist in decision-making must ensure that their systems meet strict requirements for transparency, fairness and human oversight.
18 'The proof of the pudding is in the eating' is a classic proverb meaning the true value or quality of something can only be judged when it's put to use or tested practically. It's often shortened today to 'the proof is in the pudding'.
19 Yes, it is a real word, I checked – 'Automatable' describes something that can be done automatically, typically using machines or computers instead of human effort. It implies that a task or process is suitable for being converted into an automated system or workflow.
20 Alvin Eugene Toffler was an American writer, futurist and businessman known for his works discussing modern technologies, including the digital revolution and the communication revolution, with emphasis on their effects on cultures worldwide. He is regarded as one of the world's outstanding futurists. Toffler's book Powershift: Knowledge, Wealth and Power at the Edge of the 21st Century (1990).
21 Luddites were 19th-century English textile workers who violently protested against new automated machinery, fearing job losses and wage reductions due to the introduction of power looms and other labour-saving devices. The movement, originating in Nottinghamshire in 1811, spread to other parts of England, including Yorkshire and Lancashire. They were named after a mythical figure, Ned Ludd, who was said to have smashed machinery in the 1770s.
22 John Michael 'Ozzy' Osbourne was an English singer, songwriter and media personality. He rose to prominence during the 1970s as the lead vocalist of the heavy metal band Black Sabbath, during which period he adopted the nickname 'Prince of Darkness'. RIP Ozzy.

Chapter 9

Project Darwinism, the survival of the AI adopters

9.1 Big questions (2022 and 2025)

Back in 2022 I posed what I described at the time as five really important, or at the very least intriguing questions, that we should be debating right now in project management, and they went along the lines of 'can anyone do project management in an AI empowered project world?'.

I also asked, 'In the AI project world, will certifications and qualifications of today be irrelevant?'.

I considered whether methodology would be a thing of history if AI can enable project managers in a significant way as is predicted in the future, and, kind of associated with that was, 'Will project management bodies of knowledge exist in an AI cloud of data driven intelligence, rather than in the current sort of disparate, siloed manner?'. And finally, the fifth question was, 'In an AI project world, will the skill set of the project manager be devalued?'.

9.1.1 I explored each of these in 2022

Can anyone do project management in the AI-empowered world?

> I argued that if AI is going to grab the kind of significant levels of project-based activity and do it effectively, then this will indeed allow for projects to be managed by the machine, to a very significant extent. And what that would do is it would lead those that deliver projects as projects, the dedicated project managers using the AI as their supportive partner, and will instead heavily focus their skills, their experience and their time on the people side of things. And perhaps those who deliver kind of projects as usual, which are the smaller scale, the less complex, the less risky, will significantly rely on AI to not only aid but to do the majority of the work for them. Added to which, because their needs are simpler, smaller in scale, less people intensive, they will have no need

DOI: 10.4324/9781003672357-9

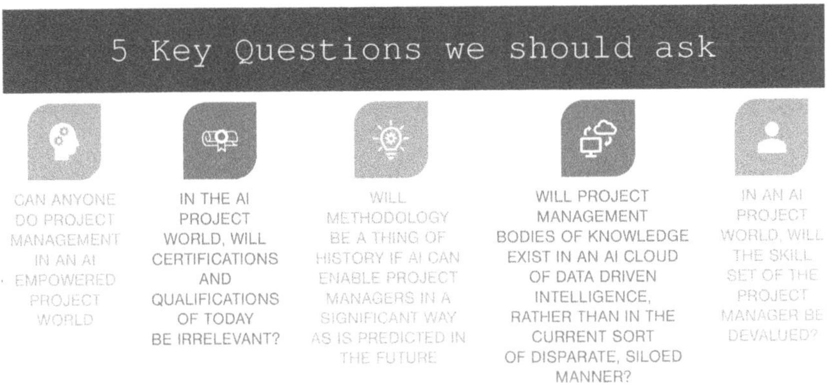

Figure 9.1 key questions we should ask.

of a project management type role or be led by someone with any great project skill or experience. So a bit of a mixed answer to that one.

Will certifications be valueless within the AI project world?

If AI is taking more and more of the job and AI does not need to be trained or certified or qualified in the sense that it is self-teaching, self-learning, then really there is no qualification required. It will always be up to date and evolving in an ever-improving manner. One of the problems with certifications is that they get out of date, don't they? So the question is what's the purpose or the value of any of the current existing certifications in this future state? A little cheekily, I then listed two pages with two columns per page of all of the incredible range of certifications that you could undertake within project management. There is a whole bucket load all competing for your interest (and your money).

And I also made the point, and I stand by this, that part of the reason we have so many certifications is it's a money-making machine. And I quoted, and this was just one example of course, but PMI, according to their August 2020 annual reports in 2020 had 1.6 million certifications registered worldwide. And I quickly extrapolated that if you take the average certification test at today's costs, that doesn't include the retest, it gives a revenue of over $800 million which is just huge.

And how will organisations like PMI, like IPMA, etc., transform their certification-based revenue flows and associated certifications and standards to be relevant and more valuable to the individual project manager and the market in general? What we've seen so far is what

> they're doing is extending education into the AI themed world, but I'm not sure, and you never know what's going on behind the scenes of course, but I'm not sure that they are thinking of what this future state is really going to look like. So it's possible that this will all change, but we don't know.

Will we abandon methodology for it become a thing of history when AI enables project managers in the future?

> Smart organisations have long moved away from methodology towards a framework that encourages flexible working, and in this sense, I think that we, and I argued at the time that we will still need some sort of guidance, some sort of structure, but it's possible that the methodology that we know today will be superseded by a kind of process-based environment, to a data-driven model, where we will use artificial intelligence, machine learning, natural language processing and so on.
>
> I recognise this could be the beginning of the death of methodology, and therefore the methodology custodians, and I suggested it was perhaps a chance to open up the world of project management to a truly global audience with no false barriers set to restrict and control or indeed profit from.

So that led on to the professional bodies question: Are they relevant?

> They could be relevant, but in what way will they, as the current custodians of such communities, how are they even thinking about in which way they're going to be relevant in the future?
>
> You know, if the technology is assuming so much, then what is the role of professional organisations in the future?

All of these questions really lead to the fifth and final question, which is, in the AI project management world, will our skills be devalued?

> I thought that there would be, to a degree, not a devaluation, perhaps, but a kind of offering of project management to the masses, to the community, to the business world, just to be a part and parcel of a basic responsibility. Common skills for anyone in business so that they can, with the aid of AI technology, run a small project without worrying about understanding project management from start to finish, just the basic principles.
>
> Now I think it does depend on the category of projects that you're talking about, but if we're talking of a moderately common, repeatable deployment of technology, that kind of thing, then, yes, I think then the

technology is going to lead the way and effectively what you've got is just the human-in-the-loop scenario for the critical/experience needed intervention.

The second question around certifications and qualifications should be what are they actually for? A test of capability (allegedly) and a proof point of future performance and competence.

But why would you have a certification or a qualification in project management if the technology is doing the majority of the project management for you? In the age of the fully automated project manager, who's going to need to be certified? And what value would it even deliver?

You know, this is an evolutionary dead end, as far as I'm concerned.[1]

9.1.2 *Looking again in 2025*

Can anyone do project management in the AI empowered world?

Pretty much, yes.

Even more convinced that this will be the case (otherwise why would I write this book?). AI is progressing at a speed that is going to overwhelm many professions, and project management is in no way except or ring-fenced from this tsunami of revolution.

Will certifications be valueless within the AI project world?

Yes.

A slight qualification perhaps in that I will discuss later in this book some new roles that I think will emerge, so maybe that's where the path goes for some form of certification or qualification. But I don't believe it's in the world of project management, for sure, at least not for the majority, but there are always, of course, going to be exceptions. There are still going to be those challenging projects, difficult projects that are going to have the human leadership. In these instances, you will want a proven, experienced and qualified person at the helm.

Will we abandon methodology for it becomes a thing of history when AI enables project managers in the future?

Yes, because this will be embedded inside the technology, inside the artificial intelligence, it's learning already, it's evolving. In my own organisation, we produce three versions or three updates to our methodology every year, incorporating significant evolutions, changes, improvements, corrections and all of that. And we do that because we recognise that methodology, or our framework, is a very dynamic beast, and as such, we need to keep it up to date. We get hundreds of points of feedback from people around the world to improve our existing methodology, and we review and respond to them all. But there is always a lag.

Now with the world of AI it is going to learn in the moment from each individual project activity, and it's going to instantaneously offer up lessons learned, and that's something we've always been really bad at, isn't it, gathering those lessons learned and sharing those lessons learned. So yes, I do believe methodology, as we know it, will be a thing of history.

Will the bodies of knowledge continue to have value?

Every organisation struggles when they put together some form of body of knowledge, some sort of defined discipline. They struggle because they can't keep it up to date. Right now there are years in between the publications of bodies of knowledge, and typically a year or more of lag once a new body of knowledge has been released for the certification, the qualification and the supporting training follows up behind it.

Just think about that. Is that going to work in the world of artificial intelligence, in the world of the fully automated project manager? Like hell it is. It's going to be pointless. They're never going to keep up, so they might as well give up instead.

In the AI project world, will the skillset of the project manager be devalued?

I'm not sure devalued is the right answer, but it will become, to a degree, invisible.

Hence my argument for the invisible project manager; it will be just like anything else that you use inside your business, your organisation or any piece of technology that helps you in your day-to-day work. It would no longer be the critical pivotal point or skill anymore.

I acknowledge that this isn't going to be the case everywhere. I believe there will always be a smaller community, a significantly smaller community, of project managers who will be highly valued. It's probably a very good job in the future to get yourself into that elite group, that particular niche.

The real question is what happens to the majority of people who are currently in project management as and when this revolution takes place.

> It is not the strongest of the species that survives, nor the most intelligent, but the one most responsive to change.
>
> Charles Darwin (attributed)

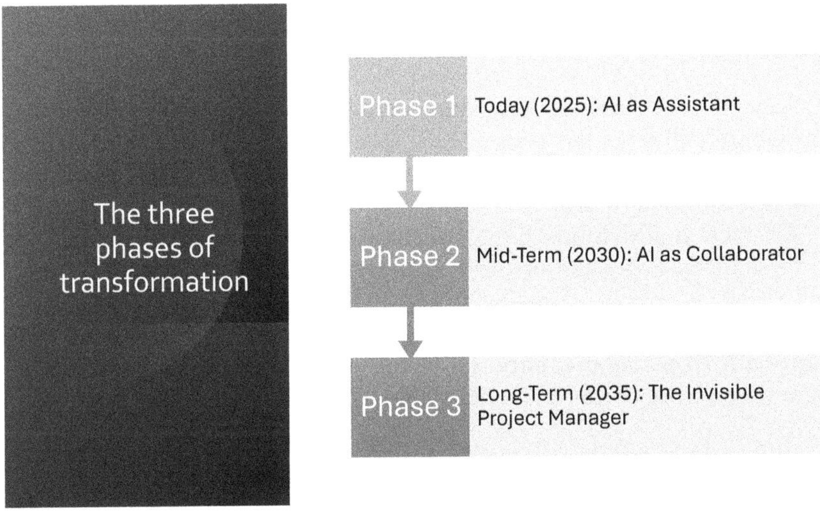

Figure 9.2 The three phases of transformation.

9.2 The three phases of transformation

Of course this is not going to happen overnight or be an instant transformation from the now to the fully automated project management world; it is going to take some time, and it won't be a smooth and untroubled progression.

As I think about how this might play out ('might' being the operative word here), you could consider the progression in three significant stages or phases.

9.2.1 *Phase 1 – today (2025): AI as assistant*

Let's start where we are right now. In 2025, artificial intelligence is not running your projects; we all know that, but it's certainly open to making your life easier.

AI tools today are brilliant at handling what I lovingly call the boring bits, or the project drudgery. Scheduling meetings, forecasting timelines, documenting requirements, tracking actions, updating reports, blah, blah, blah? All potentially automated thanks to tools like Microsoft Copilot,[2] Jira AI[3] and a swathe of LLMs.[4]

But let's not get ahead of ourselves too much; what about leadership, conflict resolution, ethical judgement and inspiring a team to keep delivering when the chips are down? That still takes a human, someone with experience, empathy and a good cup of coffee when needed.

Key characteristics of the Assistant Era:

- Principles: AI informs decisions but doesn't make value judgements; humans still drive the 'why'.
- Performance Domains: Planning and measurement will be augmented but not owned by AI.
- Artefacts and Methods: Expect documentation, dashboards and metrics to be increasingly automatically generated and updated.

The project manager, in this phase, is still very much the conductor, perhaps with AI as the orchestra. Powerful, precise, but needing a baton to follow (see more of this analogy in Chapter 10).

9.2.2 Phase 2 – mid-term (2030): AI as collaborator

Fast forward a few years to 2030 when AI isn't just your diligent assistant; it's now your full-time project partner. The shift here is subtle but seismic.

In this phase, AI doesn't just execute tasks; it makes proactive suggestions, it adapts delivery lifecycles mid-flight, it initiates stakeholder communication and runs multiple live simulations for risk. The AI understands context, senses sentiment and brace yourself, can even prioritise based on predicted stakeholder reactions.

Key characteristics of the Collaborator Era:

- Tailoring in Real Time: AI modifies project methods as the environment shifts, and it does so automatically.
- Stakeholder Engagement: From diary management to mood modelling, AI knows when to chase and when to charm.
- Quality and Risk Control: AI will be constantly correcting, optimising and updating.

What's left for the humans?

- Navigating ethical dilemmas.
- Leading with empathy.
- Managing the complex (digital) dance between humans and machines.

Here, the project manager becomes more of a steward, less about controlling delivery, more about curating success, with AI driving the train.

9.2.3 *Phase 3 – long-term (2035): The Invisible Project Manager*

By 2035, the idea of a visibly present, traditionally structured project manager will be disappearing at speed.

AI will have matured into a full-spectrum delivery engine overseeing everything from strategy execution to benefit realisation and constantly optimising for outcomes and responding to changes before you've had your first coffee of the morning.

Key characteristics of the Invisible Era:

- Principles: AI owns quality, risk and adaptability.
- Performance Domains: Planning and execution become dynamic and real-time, directed by contextual data and historical learnings.
- Methods and Models: Tailoring becomes instantaneous as AI builds the method, refines the model and applies it seamlessly.

9.2.4 *A closing thought*

Right now, in 2025, AI is the bright-eyed intern, smart, fast and helpful, but still needing your sign-off on the tricky stuff.

By 2030, it's the savvy colleague reading the room, tweaking the plan and managing half the meeting before you've spoken.

And by 2035, it's the quietly brilliant engine running everything behind the curtain.

So yes, you may become The Invisible Project Manager.

But if you've read this far, you'll know that invisibility is just another word for efficiency and in the spirit of lazy productive brilliance, isn't that exactly where we wanted to end up?

9.3 The years of conflict

Let's now jump into my time machine for a moment, shall we, come on it is perfectly safe and, let's face it, every project manager has always wanted a time machine.

We will visit the future. Only ten years into the future, so hold on tight; it is going to be a wild ride.

> *Change is hard and resistance is natural, but progress is inevitable, especially when it means doing less and achieving more.*
>
> (Peter Taylor – *The Lazy Project Manager*)

Ah, the timeless tale of two tribes, no, not the Montagues and Capulets,[5] instead I am talking about the early adopters and the traditionalists. Those who will sprint towards the future like it's a Black Friday sale on AI tools, and those who will doggedly cling to their beloved PMBOK guide like it's a flotation device in a sea of change.

This conflicting future tale of tension, turf wars and technological tantrums will, in my humble opinion, define the next decade in our profession.

To be honest I don't have a time machine, I don't have a crystal ball, and I don't have any magical insight into what will be, but I have a strong suspicion that it will be something along these lines.

9.3.1 Riding the wave

Let's talk about one of technology's favourite habits: Arriving in waves and not gentle, sandy waves but more like massive, world-altering, tsunami-scale tidal waves.

Everett Rogers' Diffusion of Innovations,[6] which neatly breaks the world into five types of adopters, each playing a role in how innovation goes from a dawn through to a convergence, provides further insight.

Rogers provides the distribution of the five adopter categories as follows: Innovators represent the first 2.5% of the group to adopt an innovation, followed by 13.5% as early adopters, 34% as early majorities, 34% as late majorities, and finally, 16% as laggards.

And here's the kicker in that you can't drag the laggards or force the late majority or rush the early majority, but you can plan for the curve, recognise where you are and build the road to the new future.

Right, with that in mind, let's now look into that future.

9.3.2 2025: Dawn of the divide

Generative AI is everywhere writing emails, summarising meetings, building project schedules and even flagging risks before your sponsor does.

The early AI adopters are living the life exploring numerous ways to benefit from artificial intelligence.

Meanwhile, the traditionalists hold firm and grasp onto their belief in the old ways.

9.3.3 2025–2028: The challenging cold war

Debate rages, project expert panels grow tense, conferences fight for positioning affiliation, while LinkedIn and other social media become a battleground for bold claims and cautious scepticism. Two clear opposing camps rise up even though the reality was that truth is, as it often is, less 'black and white'.

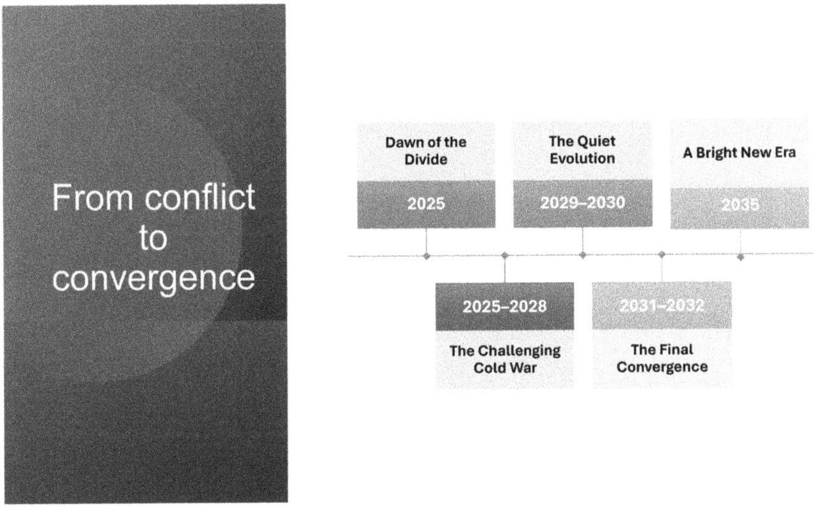

Figure 9.3 From conflict to convergence.

'Can AI really effectively run a project end-to-end?' becomes the new 'Waterfall vs Agile'[7] argument.

The early adopters perhaps underestimate the value of experience while traditionalists overestimate the permanence of their processes, with the result that neither side wins the argument as yet.

9.3.4 *2029–2030: The quiet evolution*

AI gets smarter, not just faster, but actually smarter as it starts to understand why things happen, not just what's happening.

Predictive insights become explainable and AI flags behavioural shifts, disengaged sponsors and team members, flagging and reacting to early warning signs of potential failure or high risk and all without breaking a (digital) sweat.

By 2030, the Invisible Project Manager isn't theoretical; it's running some real portfolios, in real-time.

Early adopters and early majority are deep in the new world and trying to persuade the rest to join the party.

9.3.5 *2031–2032: The final convergence*

The traditionalists begin to embrace the change and not out of fear, but out of weary acceptance.

Early adopters and early majority, along with the late majority, are seeing this new way of working as the norm. Certainly, anyone entering the workplace in the last 5 years will just not understand what all the fuss is about.

9.3.6 2035: A bright new era

Everyone is part of the new fully automated project world, and resistance has been proved futile.

Technology has won the day and rapidly people will forget about the old ways except for a wry smile from the old-timers about how hard it was in 'their day' and reflect that the new kids have it easy.

9.3.7 Final thought from an old-timer

The years of conflict weren't wasted and no doubt they were uncomfortable, for many, but they were also necessary.

Because through tension came transformation, through resistance came resilience and learning, and through just a little bit of strategic laziness finally there came progress.

CHATPBT

Back in 2022, I threw out five big questions about the future of project management – not to stir up trouble (well, maybe a little), but because it was clear things were shifting. Fast forward to 2025, and what was once speculation is now just Tuesday.

First up: Can anyone manage a project in an AI-powered world? Honestly, yes – especially if we're talking about those run-of-the-mill, rinse-and-repeat projects. AI has them covered. It plans, tracks, updates, nudges... probably makes the tea too. What's left for us humans is the messy, unpredictable stuff – dealing with people, interpreting nuance, calming the chaos. So no, not everyone's out of a job, but the job has definitely changed. The project manager isn't centre stage anymore. More like the director in the wings, quietly making sure it all doesn't fall apart.

Then there's certification. Once the golden ticket, now... a little tarnished. If AI is doing most of the heavy lifting and learning on the fly, what's the point of us collecting paper certificates like scout badges? I'm not saying learning is dead – far from it – but maybe we need to rethink what actually proves value. Spoiler alert: It's probably not another four-letter acronym after your name.

Methodology? Don't get me started. We used to argue over Waterfall vs Agile like it was a religious debate. Now, AI just shrugs and says, 'I'll take what works, thanks'. It doesn't care what your slide deck says. It looks at what actually delivers results and adapts on the fly.

And those big, dusty bodies of knowledge we used to pore over like sacred scrolls? They simply can't keep up. AI updates in real time. It learns from every project, every outcome, every blip on the radar. Meanwhile, the human-written versions take years to refresh, and by the time they do, the world has moved on. It's not that they're wrong. They're just… slow.

So, is the project manager's skillset being devalued? Not quite. It's being redistributed. The stuff that made us indispensable – process, structure, control – is being handled by machines. What's left are the things that machines still can't do well: Empathy, trust, leadership without a Gantt Chart. In a way, we're becoming less visible, but maybe more valuable.

This change won't come with a big bang. First, AI will help out. Then it will become a partner. Soon, for many projects, it'll be driving the whole thing – with us riding shotgun, offering occasional course corrections and making sure the humans still feel like humans.

Of course, some people will be clinging to the old ways – gripping their PMBOK like it's a lifebuoy on a sinking ship. Others, though, will have already handed the reins to AI and are sipping coffee while their virtual assistant flags a scope creep. I get it. Change is hard. But if progress means doing less and getting more… well, that's got 'productively lazy' written all over it.

We won't lose control. We'll lose the illusion that we ever had it in the first place. How wonderfully lazy is that?

Notes

1 Another dinosaur situation maybe.

2 Microsoft Copilot is an AI companion designed to assist with various tasks, acting as a digital assistant across different Microsoft platforms and devices. It is available for both personal and professional use, helping with tasks like research, writing, coding and even creative tasks like image generation.

3 A suite of artificial intelligence (AI) features integrated into Jira project and issue tracking software. These features aim to streamline workflows, automate tasks and enhance productivity within Jira to assist with tasks like issue creation, summarisation, knowledge base management and agent assignment in Jira Service Management.

4 Top five at the time of writing – GPT-4o – OpenAI, Claude 3.5 Opus – Anthropic, Gemini 1.5 Pro – Google DeepMind, Mixtral 8x7B – Mistral, LLaMA 3 70B – Meta.

5 In William Shakespeare's Romeo and Juliet, the Montagues and Capulets are two prominent families engaged in a bitter feud. This conflict forms the backdrop of the tragic love story between Romeo Montague and Juliet Capulet.

6 Everett Rogers' Diffusion of Innovations theory explains how, why, and at what rate new ideas and technologies spread through cultures. It identifies five key elements that influence the adoption process: The innovation itself, communication channels, time, the social system and the adopter categories.

7 Which is probably still raging amongst the few.

Chapter 10

The future is not managing, it's orchestrating

10.1 The movement of change

If this vision becomes a reality, what is left for the 'human' to do in the fully automated project management world?

Will it be the end of the need for people, or will the roles required evolve into something else?

Let's explore this in two ways. One is to consider a view of project management from a few years ago, an analogy with music, a rock band to be precise. And the second is a consideration of an evolution of roles that would elevate the human contribution to where it matters most.

10.2 Rock star PM

Some time ago I wrote an article on the idea of project management being musically aligned and with the project manager being some sort of musician in a rock band.

The idea of the piece was to support a presentation that I was doing (always available for customised, insightful and yet fun keynotes) and the imagery of a rock band is understood by pretty much everyone.

Anyway the piece went like this:

> *Music is a very personal matter; as I write this, I am listening to the band Golden Earring playing 'Radar Love'*[1]*'(perhaps the finest pop/rock single ever produced… see you are already disagreeing with me, it is a personal choice after all, I know that).*
>
> *Rockstar*
>
> *But musical taste aside, if you take a fairly typical four-piece pop/rock band it commonly consists of a drummer, a bass player, a lead guitarist and a vocalist.*

DOI: 10.4324/9781003672357-10

The drummer provides a steady beat and emphasises the other instruments and vocals, perhaps with the occasional solo where they have full control of the flow and style of the music being played. The drummer can be very influential within a band.

The bass player has the crucial role in the band and the group members depend on the bassist's subtle lead. If the guitarist or drummer makes a mistake it can easily going unnoticed but if the bassist makes a mistake, everyone will instantly know that something is wrong.

The lead guitarist is one of the most important contributors in a band, whether they just add in riffs here and there or play mesmerising guitar solos. There is an added attraction to the role in that they are typically second only to the lead vocalist when it comes to fame, spotlight, and all that comes with that.

Finally the lead vocalist is the most often the main focus of the audience's attention. This is due partly to the fact that the front person is interpreting the lyrics which make up the story of the song and partly due to the singers' charisma.

Now consider your style as a project manager, which one are you?

- *A 'drummer' offering a steady backbeat to keep the rhythm of the project on track?*
- *A 'bassist' keeping the team together, ensuring that no mistakes are made?*
- *A 'lead guitarist' adding in inspirational leadership moments and creativity?*
- *A 'vocalist' interpreting the vision of the project and being the figurehead?*

Or perhaps you play more than one role.

Neat, eh? Well it was certainly a 'hit' (see what I did there?) with the audience and with many people sharing additional thoughts after I posted it online.

10.3 Rockstar rewired

Now let me update this into the state of fully automated project management and we will see how it 'plays' out (see what I did again there?).

As I write this, I am listening to the messy genius of Golden Earring's Radar Love and my personal go-to if I have writer's block song that is the mighty Metallica[2] and 'For Whom the Bell's Tolls' and 'Enter Sandman'. AI music will never be like this surely.

- The drummer provides rhythm and stability.
- The bassist keeps the band grounded and steady.
- The lead guitarist injects solos and bursts of creativity.
- The vocalist interprets the song's story as typically owning the spotlight.

Genius creativity comes from band tensions and passion, but what happens to this musical analogy in a world where the band is entirely non-human, entirely automated?

Now every beat, every chord and every line of the lyrics is generated in real time by AI technology that references perfect musical theory and has digital insights into audience sentiment, is totally up to date on current music trends and the whole delivery is technically flawless with the tempo being precise, the transitions being seamless and the harmonies mathematically beautiful. Add to that no beat is missed and no note ever off-key.

- The drummer is now a real-time scheduling algorithm adjusting timelines based on dependencies, risks and real-world events faster than any human could tap a hi-hat.
- The bassist is a predictive analytics engine quietly monitoring project health, resourcing and scope creep and alerting the system before anything becomes audible to stakeholders.
- The guitarist is a creative AI surfacing innovative delivery approaches, optimising user stories and simulating outcomes with flair (but without ego).
- The vocalist is the generative interface summarising progress, articulating vision, tailoring updates for stakeholders and delivering them in perfectly pitched tones.

It's all orchestrated #nobandneeded.

If the 'band' is now fully automated, what role is left for you, the human, in the equation.

You're no longer the drummer or the bassist, the guitarist or the singer since the FAPM plays all roles, all the time, and does so flawlessly and tirelessly. Musical differences are now (and forever) a thing of the past and comebacks are irrelevant, as this band will never go away.

I went to see 'Abba Voyage'[3] not so long ago, and it was totally amazing. This is a concert experience in London where digital avatars of the pop group ABBA[4] perform alongside a live 'human' band, using cutting-edge technology. The avatars (or abbatars as the joke goes) are based on the group's likeness from 1977, created using motion capture technology. The show features a setlist of their greatest hits.

The live musician lead joked that this was the toughest gig ever as Abba were perfect night after night (no surprise there) and this put intense pressure on the live musicians to match the quality levels.

It was, as I said, amazing, and it was perfect, and it was a huge amount of fun, but would I like to see all concerts[5] like this – probably not, but it delivered and it was entertaining, and think about it: It can scale globally – the band, any band, could be playing live in multiple cities at the same time.

Anyway, I digress slightly; the question asked was, 'what role is left to you the human?'

Well, instead, maybe you're now the producer defining the vision of the album, curating the right emotional tone, setting goals for success and choosing the genre for each 'project track'.

Or perhaps you're the label executive aligning the music (projects) with audience (customer) needs and business strategy.

Or maybe you're the audience, finally free to focus on outcomes rather than process, just listening to what's being delivered and deciding if it resonates.

The fully automated band never misses a beat, but someone still needs to define what song to play and why it matters.

Perhaps that's the future of project leadership.

Rock on!

10.4 Life after the PM

Let's assume, for argument's sake, that the rise of AI in project management has led to the emergence of the Invisible Project Manager (FAPM) as I am predicting in this book.

While some of you might fear this would make human roles obsolete, the reality is probably far more nuanced since rather than replacing people, AI will now be reshaping project work to elevate human contribution where it matters most: In creativity, ethics, empathy and strategic thinking.

Taking this position as it is, let's explore the potential new human roles that will thrive in the AI-powered project world.

To be clear here, this is conceptual projection on my part; the reality will be what it needs to be, but I believe such forward thinking can help you all navigate towards a future career adaptation.

10.4.1 Project orchestrator

Role Summary: This role is about guiding the AI towards the strategic stage; the technology manages the notes, but you're holding the baton, ensuring what's played matches the business tune.

10.4.2 *Experience designer*

Role Summary: This role makes sure people feel part of the show and not just audience spectators to a machine performance.

10.4.3 *Outcome navigator*

Role Summary: This impresario role steers towards value, ensuring the AI performs successfully.

10.4.4 *Collaboration coach*

Role Summary: This role focuses on the digital dancing to the catchy tune where people and machines work together in a positive and productive manner.

10.4.5 *Digital ethics and Governance officer*

Role Summary: Someone has to keep the AI honest (no musical plagiarism here) and this role ensures the technology is fair, transparent, and complies with all legal and moral expectations.

10.4.6 *Trust architect*

Role Summary: People won't follow what they don't trust; therefore, this role makes sure AI doesn't just work, but it is promoted in a safe, fair and clear manner.

10.5 The new band

If we consider these new emergent roles, then this could form the basis of the FAPM world PMO.

In this world the new style (AI)PMO doesn't manage projects in the old sense, but it ensures AI-driven delivery aligns with strategic, ethical and human-centred priorities.

Here's what this modern PMO might look like:

- Project Orchestrators guide and calibrate the AI engines, ensuring projects stay aligned with business goals and adapting systems as strategies evolve.
- Experience Designers keep the workplace emotionally intelligent, turning machine-led updates into meaningful human conversations and keeping people engaged.

- Outcome Navigators focus on value, not just output, translating business needs into AI-executable goals, and validating whether the work delivers impact.
- Collaboration Coaches help humans and machines work in sync, upskilling teams to prompt, interpret and partner with AI systems effectively.
- Trust Architects build confidence in the system, maintaining transparency, encouraging feedback and ensuring users feel secure.

The Digital Ethics and Governance Officers (most likely centralised business resource) will provide the conscience of the PMO, ensuring transparency, fairness and regulatory alignment in all AI-driven actions.

It's the team behind the machine, ensuring automation doesn't lose its humanity, and that strategy, empathy and ethics stay front and centre.

10.6 The human advantage

The Invisible Project Manager doesn't mean the end of project professionals, but it will definitely signal the evolution of their purpose and work focus.

In this new FAPM world, humans are not micromanagers but visionaries, ethicists, translators and designers of meaningful work.

As machines take care of the 'how' we can return to the 'why' and 'who', and the future state PMO will need to be very different as well, becoming the 'team behind the machine'.

The future of project management is not less human; it is just different and demands new skills.

CHATPBT

Once upon a time, the project manager was the rock star. Sometimes the drummer, keeping the beat. Sometimes the bassist, holding the team together. Sometimes the lead guitarist, bringing flair. And sometimes the vocalist, telling the story and owning the spotlight.

But in a world of Fully Automated Project Management – the FAPM – that band has gone digital. AI now keeps perfect rhythm, catches risks before they appear, simulates creative options and delivers polished updates to stakeholders without breaking a sweat.

No band needed.

So what happens to us humans? Are we out of the tour bus?

Not quite.

Maybe now we become the producer – shaping the vision, tone and direction. Or the label exec – aligning delivery with customer needs. Or even the audience – finally free to judge the outcome instead of managing the chaos.

Better still, new roles are emerging.

We become orchestrators, experience designers, outcome navigators, collaboration coaches, ethics officers, storytellers and trust builders.

Because while the FAPM takes care of the how, we get to focus on the why.

Project management is not dying. It is evolving. And if you're ready to stop playing every note and start writing the next album, the future is wide open.

Notes

1 'Radar Love' is a song by the Dutch rock band Golden Earring.
2 'For Whom the Bell Tolls' is a song by American thrash metal band Metallica. It was first released on their second studio album, *Ride the Lightning* (1984).
3 https://abbavoyage.com/
4 ABBA were a Swedish pop group formed in Stockholm in 1972 by Agnetha Fältskog, Björn Ulvaeus, Benny Andersson and Anni-Frid Lyngstad. They are among the most renowned and commercially successful musical groups in history, ranking as one of the bestselling acts in the history of popular music.
5 Rock band KISS and UK girl band, the Spice Girls are among others thinking of following this path.

Chapter 11

The invisible project manager manifesto

11.1 The 10 principles for a FAPM future

by Peter Taylor *(The ultimate lazy project manager)*

In a world shaped by automation, intelligence and accelerated delivery, the traditional project manager is no longer the hero (sorry but you have to deal with it), because now it is all about the project.

Welcome to the era of 'The Invisible Project Manager'.

Here are the ten principles that could well define this shift:

Don't resist the invisible project manager future. Design it and be part of it.

Table 11.1 Ten principles that have led to *The Invisible Project Manager*

Projects should manage themselves	If it can be tracked, updated or escalated then it can be automated. The system should do the managing; humans should do the thinking, but that thinking should be designed to be the absolute bare minimum.
Visibility is the new control	Real-time dashboards driven by live data replace subjective progress updates, providing insight not oversight. Stakeholders have continuous visibility into project health without needing to ask supported by reporting by exception only when there are non-recoverable deviations of project progress.
Governance should be embedded, not enforced	Trust the process, literally. Governance lives in workflows, in automations, and in intelligent alerts, not in reviews and signoffs.
The team should lead Itself	With the right structure, clarity and tools, teams can effectively self-regulate. Leadership becomes distributed with teams becoming their own architects of autonomy.
Meetings are merely a symptom of failure	If a project relies on frequent check-ins, then it is compensating for what is a poor workflow and unclear ownership. Silence is progress.

(Continued)

DOI: 10.4324/9781003672357-11

Table 11.1 (Continued)

Projects should manage themselves	If it can be tracked, updated or escalated then it can be automated. The system should do the managing; humans should do the thinking, but that thinking should be designed to be the absolute bare minimum.
Outcome over activity wins	Focus shifts from tracking tasks and micromanaging timelines to delivering real business value. Success is measured by impact only.
Human effort should focus on innovation, not administration	Free your smartest people from tracking work so they can improve it. Admin is for algorithms.
Stakeholder-centric engagement is key	Engagement strategies are tailored and optimised through AI insights. Communication is proactive, personalised and automatically adjusted for impact and sentiment.
Dynamic, adaptive planning drives progress	Plans are living entities, updated constantly by machine learning algorithms reacting to project conditions. The days of static, front-loaded planning are over because now fluidity is a feature and not a flaw.
Continuous learning and evolution at all times	AI learns from every project, improving future performance autonomously. PMOs evolve into centres of excellence for learning loops, not control towers.

CHATPBT

Hey there, future-focused folks!

In 'The 10 Principles for a FAPM (Fully Automated Project Manager) Future' by Peter Taylor (aka The Ultimate Lazy Project Manager*), we're stepping into the era of The Invisible Project Manager – where humans aren't running the show, the project is. Sorry traditional PMs, it's not about you anymore.*

So what's the deal? Well, if something can be tracked or escalated, it can – and should – be automated. Real-time dashboards? Yep, they're replacing those painful status meetings. Governance? It's baked into smart workflows now, not buried in bureaucratic signoffs. Teams will just lead themselves, meetings are a red flag, and silence equals progress (no news is good news, literally).

We're measuring impact, not activity. Admin work? That's AI territory. Humans should focus on innovation, not updating spreadsheets. Planning is now adaptive and alive, constantly reshaped by AI. And PMOs? They're evolving into learning hubs, not control freaks.

The future is here. Invisible doesn't mean irrelevant – it means intelligent. Don't fight it. Design it. Own it.

Chapter 12

Not a single evolutionary path

12.1 When two tribes go to war

I made a declarative statement at the start of this book: *'My belief and declaration is that in the near (much nearer than most people think) future, the dedicated role of the project manager (in many project scenarios) will vanish and be replaced by AI-driven orchestration instead'*.

I realise and spoke about this in the chapter on project Darwinism and the likely rough journey from conflict to convergence when there will be, inevitably, two major tribes or groups – the pro AI and the anti AI. So perhaps this next chapter will bring some calmness to any hot-blooded angst or anger out there.

The biggest question of all is, I would humbly suggest, does all this fully automated project manager stuff mean that there is just one outcome from all of this, or one path on the journey?

No, I don't think so. There will be two project worlds, depending on the scale, complexity and risk.

How did I conclude that?

Well, let us just take an imaginary walk through a future state debate for our profession and just see where we end up.

Welcome to a conversation from inside my own mind on this topic (I was on a transatlantic flight at the time and I threw my basic thoughts down while whiling away the hours – just think, had there been a decent film on then this whole thing might not have existed and you would have been rescued from having to read this).

12.2 The debate

Thought 1:

My argument is this that whilst an advocate of the project management profession for many years, I have become increasingly convinced that the

DOI: 10.4324/9781003672357-12

future of project management will be fundamentally different to that of today, and that is thanks primarily to the rise of AI Artificial Intelligence.

My belief and declaration is that in the near, probably much nearer than most people think, future, the dedicated role of the project manager in the majority of project scenarios will vanish and be replaced by the AI-driven orchestration stage.

This is what I define as the invisible project manager: The future where AI systems silently, seamlessly manage workflow, timelines, resources, and the human-in-the-loop will require a vastly different skill set, moving from the managers of activities to the guardians of outcomes. The bottom line here is that fully automated project management is possible now because we have the computational capability to process vast amounts of data in real time. We also have the AI to interpret attacks on information intelligently and without previous rules or code, and it's getting better all the time. Plus, we have the connected systems to monitor and coordinate work automatically, and, actually, we also have the cultural readiness or openness to trust automation for project management functions.

So that's my position on this one. What do you think?

Thought 2:
Well, it's a bold claim certainly, but here's a counter challenge in that AI might simulate 90% of what project managers do but it will not simulate what project managers are. Big difference I feel.

I mean, project management isn't about the task tracking, the reporting or the scheduling. It's about influence, it's about judgment, it's about conflict resolution and it's about navigating ambiguity. These are deeply human domains that AI may automate the mechanics, but managing stakeholders, resolving human tensions and making ethical decisions in real time. That's not automation territory. That's leadership.

Thought 1:
So really, you don't believe that most of this can be done in some way by AI in the very near future.

Thought 2:
Okay, I'll concede that some of it can, and I can break that down.

For example, AI can monitor tasks and deadlines, generate reports and forecasts, optimise resource identification and allocation and even identify risk-based patterns.

But think about this.

What about negotiating with an angry client who's threatening to cancel the project or escalate this to senior management or walk away from the project completely?

What about rebuilding a team morale after a failed sprint or a major issue or stumbling block?

What about interpreting political undertones in a stakeholder request, not taking it at face value, understanding what's behind it, what's driving that question, what's driving that decision? What's driving that position of difficulty?

What about deciding when not to follow the data just because your gut says something quite not right? Something's off. It's just human instinct.

So AI can simulate professionalism, but it can't simulate presence. It can model empathy, but it can't feel it. And leadership often hinges on exactly those soft barrels.

So let me summarise. AI can do some version of 90% for sure, but does that 90% actually result in successful project delivery, especially, and here's the key, especially in messy, difficult, complex political high-stakes, high-risk environments.

Thought 1:
Okay, what if we took the people mostly out of the equation? Then you don't get a lot of these issues, do you?

Thought 2:
Now, that's a very different battlefield. That's a very different landscape. You're not just automating the project manager. You're reimagining the project environment itself.

If we remove, or we drastically reduce the human element, the human content, if you like things like clients, stakeholders, team members, all of that, if we then replace them with AI agents, if we replace them with digital workflows, and if we replace them with autonomous systems, then, yeah, context. That context becomes machine manageable. You've removed conflict, you've removed ambiguity, you removed emotion. All that messy, messy stuff, all of it will dramatically decline. But here's the rebuttal, projects exist to change or create value for people. You yourself have always said projects are about people.

Even if AI builds absolutely everything, it still builds it for someone, and that someone brings missing this back into the system. It's really hard to avoid that. So unless this future state model includes entirely machine-driven projects from initiation to delivery with no stakeholder expectations, no human governance, no emotional response to outcomes, no people. You will still need a layer of leadership that understands people for them to be in any way successful or useful, valuable.

So tell me this, are you saying, are you suggesting that we will change the nature of projects themselves? Or are you just saying we'll automate how projects are managed today?

Big question.

Thought 1:

I believe in many cases that the nature of projects will inevitably change. Technology will lead us in this new direction.

Thought 2:

Now we're getting somewhere.

If the nature of projects changes, so too must the nature of project management, and I think that is your real argument. What you're envisioning here is a world where AI designs and scopes the project based on real-time business signals. AI assembles teams. Most of those will be actually synthetic agents and not people. AI adjusts execution dynamically, guided by continuous feedback loops, and AI's involvement, therefore, is minimal. It's just confined to oversight and it's confined to outcome consumption. In that world, the classic or traditional project manager isn't just invisible. They're absolutely obsolete.

Let me counter again, even if projects evolve into highly automated AI to AI systems, there will be still moments of uncertainty, times of demanding innovation and moments of disruption that no model has ever seen, and historical data will not help you overcome that. That is something that demands human experience.

That's when you'll need someone to break the model, to ask those uncomfortable questions or challenge the system's assumptions. That's when you need someone to lead. When the system can't, the system can never leave. The system can manage. The system can deliver, but it cannot lead in that sense. Therefore, the question is, yes, is your invisible project manager adaptable in chaos if it hasn't been trained on because, let's face it, humans still excel at thinking sideways, thinking outside the box. As a common statement, this is something humans are brilliant at. And projects don't always naturally go forward. Sometimes they go sideways, sometimes they go backwards, sometimes they go up, they go down, they go in every single direction, but the one you originally thought they were going to go in. So now, convince me that artificial intelligence could not just manage the known, could actually lead through the unknown as well.

Thought 1:
It can't, I'll be honest, it can't, but also, I come from a world, and there are many like me where projects are highly similar. I know every project is different, every project is unique, you know, a unique endeavour, temporary, blah, blah, blah, all that kind of stuff. But I come from a world of projects that are highly similar, software deployment ones, for example, and so much more can be done in this world, I think, by the fully automated project manager.

Thought 2:
Now, that is a strong and targeted point, and that one is hard to refute, because you're right in that many modern projects, especially in enterprise software deployment, are highly repetitive, are extremely rules based, and are very pattern rich.

That's prime hunting ground for the Fully Automated Project Manager (FAPM) close brackets, because in these environments, the scope is templated. The timelines are often very predictable. The dependencies are known from experience. The risks typically follow recurring patterns, and in this case, the Human Project Manager becomes a glorified administrator, and that will probably offend lots of people, but that is the truth. What are they doing? Well, they're wrangling with the tools. They're pushing updates, they're chasing people, they're scheduling stand-ups, they're doing all of that administrative activity. And you know what, the fully automated project manager will be able, without a doubt, to handle all of that better, do it faster and do it without burnout. 24/7-365, they will never tire since it is not human, never, so yes, in this targeted area, or this structured project ecosystem, then you don't need empathy. Or at least you need less empathy. You don't need to handle politics. Typically, you don't necessarily need intuition. Hardly. What you need instead is consistency. What you need is speed, and what you need is precision because it is all about efficiency and delivering success as quickly as possible. And whoa, guess what? Artificial intelligence wins there. High score, no competition. AI up, humans down and in high-scale portfolios, hundreds of deployments, for example, possibly thousands of deployments, then removing humans from 90% of the delivery overhead is not just possible, it's economically irresistible. Do the math.

But here's my opinion,

If we accept that the fully automated project manager thrives in these repetitive, low-ambiguity projects, the question is: Are we building our entire project ecosystem to only support those types of projects? Because what happens to innovation projects, research and development projects, transformational projects or programs, crisis recoveries? Are those now special cases requiring hybrid models, or will the fully automated project manager eventually reach those as well?

Big, big question there. Does FAPM scale up to the edge of innovation, or do we keep a parallel system for the messy stuff?

Thought 1:

Well, I believe we will need that parallel system.

I've always argued that we operate even today with multiple levels of project management types, we have what I refer to as the 'PAP,' that is, projects as projects. This is where we need a dedicated project manager; the complexity, the risk of the project, the newness of the project, demands to have a professional project manager overseeing it. But we also see in organisations a very significant rise of what I term as 'PAU', projects as usual. This is where there is lower complexity, more simpler projects that are managed on a day-to-day basis by the management team, by the business leaders as part of their day job, and not by dedicated project managers. So I believe we're already in a world where we have parallel systems in place.

So to go back to your question about the need for parallel systems, then I think, actually, yes, we will need it. And the reason we need it is the fact that there are those two worlds out there. There are the worlds of common, highly similar (to a degree repetitive) type projects that can be, I believe, fully automated. And then there is the world of the new, the complex, the challenging, the bleeding edge, the super creative, and these then I think still need a human to lead, a human project or programme manager, but still, I think there is a massive, massive opportunity for those project managers, those programme managers, to be supported by artificial intelligence and have that technological support, that of a digital partner.

Thought 2:

Exactly now that's the inflection point as you are actually arguing for a bifurcated project future.

One stream is the fully automated project manager dominated stream, which is predictable, which is repeatable, which is cost efficient and is actively machine run. And then the other one is human led. This is where you have high stakes, you have ambiguity, you have significant degrees of creativity. You have the high-level political sensitivity, and this is the world that will be led by project managers, humans, people, but still a world increasingly supported by automated project management capabilities. And honestly, that's just not plausible; it's smart. It mirrors how we already divide labour up between automation and human ingenuity in other domains, think industrial robots versus product designs, for example.

And there is a strategic payoff in this model. First of all, you free up human talent from the project factory floor, so no more humans buried in Gantt Charts for cookie-cutter rollouts or driven into ever-increasing administrative (boring tedious overheads), and let's be honest, most people don't enjoy that. And secondly, you scale delivery without scaling headcount. The fully automated project manager can run many projects, hundreds of projects, thousands of projects potentially, in parallel and be significantly error-free.

You probably, and I think is accepted by everybody, have to have a human on stand-by ready to leap into action at some point for the moments where it will fall out of that automated process. For whatever reason, some difficulties and challenges, even some kind of customer or stakeholder escalation. But the majority can run from start to finish without heavy human intervention. And guess what? You then redeploy skilled project managers where they're actually needed, the hard stuff, the new stuff, the difficult stuff, the stuff that moves the needle. The frankly interesting stuff.

But let's close with a caution here.

If organisations adopt fully automated project management without a clear model for when human judgement is non-negotiable, then they risk over-automating, and they risk under-thinking, and they risk significant problems at a future point in time. So FAPM is a tool. It's very, very powerful, and it's an amazing future state, but it does need strategic governance, and that brings us logically into the world of the concept of what is the role of the current PMO in this future state.[1]

Thought 1:
I think we are very much on the same page.

Thought 2:
I believe that we are indeed.

Thought 1:
It is not about two paths going to war[2] but instead how best to use these parallel paths.

Thought 2:
True story.

CHATPBT

This little internal debate kicked off somewhere over the Atlantic, mid-flight, when the film selection was abysmal. So naturally, the noble author, forever productive, decided to imagine the future of project management instead. You're welcome.

At the heart of it, I made a bold claim (and I stand by it):

The traditional, dedicated project manager role will, in many scenarios, vanish – replaced by AI-driven orchestration.

Cue dramatic music.

But before we all run for the hills or start hugging our Gantt charts, let's be clear: I'm not suggesting project managers are obsolete in all cases. Quite the opposite. What I'm proposing is that we're heading towards a bifurcated project future – two distinct paths, each with its own rules of engagement.

Path 1: The Fully Automated Project Manager (FAPM)

Think enterprise software rollouts, where projects are templated, predictable and repeatable. Here, AI can shine. No messy politics, no emotional stakeholders, no one crying over scope creep at 2am.

In this world, the Fully Automated Project Manager handles the lot. AI works 24/7, doesn't take lunch breaks, and never forgets a deadline. In these structured, repetitive environments, FAPM isn't just a tool – it's an economic no-brainer. Human PMs become glorified administrators, and frankly, no one really wants that job anyway.

Path 2: The Human Project Leader

Now let's talk about the real, messy, complex stuff – innovation projects, transformation programs, crisis recoveries. The kind of work where stakeholder management, conflict resolution and political navigation aren't just handy – they're critical. AI can simulate empathy, but it can't feel it. It can model professionalism, but it can't lead. And when the system hits an unknown unknown, it's not an algorithm that's going to step up and say, 'Something's not right here'. That's still very much a human superpower.

So, verdict?

We're not choosing between AI or humans. We're embracing both – and applying them strategically.

For cookie-cutter projects? Let the machines roll.

For ambiguity, emotion and chaos? Send in the humans.

And for everything in between? Support the humans with the machines.

This isn't two paths going to war. It's two roads running in parallel, each serving their purpose, not fighting – but complementing.

And here's the kicker: This dual model lets us liberate human PMs from the tedium of tool-wrangling and put them where they're truly valuable – solving problems, making decisions and leading change. The interesting stuff. The stuff that matters.

Let's not fear the FAPM; instead, let's deploy it wisely, govern it strategically, and let humans do what only humans can do.

Notes

1 Idea for the next book maybe? The Invisible PMO?

2 Inspired by the awesome song 'Two Tribes', which is an anti-war song by the British band 'Frankie Goes to Hollywood', released in the UK by ZTT Records on 4 June 1984.

Chapter 13

Ending with a smile

We started way back at the beginning of this book with a joke. Well, I considered it a joke but humour is individual, I do realise.

Anyway, here is one to end this book which, I hope, will both make you smile and think.

A project manager walks into a boardroom with a shiny new AI assistant called ALFIE (Artificial Leadership Facilitator for Intelligent Execution).

> *Ladies and gentlemen, thank you for attendance and attention'* the project overlord says, *'ALFIE can handle every aspect of project delivery. Absolutely everything from planning, risk, budget, stakeholders, you name it and ALFIE can do it'.*

The CFO says, *'Sure, but can it manage our projects?'*

To demonstrate this immediately ALFIE is fed all necessary data for a real nightmare of a project. We are talking global rollout, 18 stakeholders, shifting scope, disappearing developers, three clashing executives and a vendor who communicates exclusively via emojis and memes.

ALFIE processes for 0.3 seconds, then generates a complete project plan, risk log, communications strategy and contingency roadmap, all colour-coded and emoji-optimised.

The boardroom audience is stunned.

Then the CIO challenges it, *'What happens when marketing wants to rebrand again, one week before launch?'*

The board all smile in a knowing manner.

ALFIE pauses, lights dim, cooling fans spin louder and within a short time it prints a single sticky note.

The CEO picks it up from the output printer and reads it aloud:

'Dear Stakeholders: No – Sincerely, the AI'.

The board member cheer as one.

'Finally', they say, *'Someone on this team understands boundaries'.*

DOI: 10.4324/9781003672357-13

Chapter 14

A final word (after the rain)

A final word (after the rain)There is a great book by Neville Shute called *In the Wet*, the storyline goes like this:

> It is the rainy season. Drunk and delirious, an old man lies dying in the Queensland bush. In his opium-hazed last hours, a priest finds his deserted shack and listens to his last words. Half-awake and half-dreaming the old man tells the story of an adventure set decades in the future, in a very different world...[1]

Right now, as I write the last few words of this book, it somehow feels similar in that I am sharing a vision of a future project world from the perspective of someone who has been in it for a number of decades now, and maybe I am right, or maybe I am completely wrong, and perhaps it will be something of a halfway house.

Who knows?

Perhaps it is just a story or maybe an illusion.

Time, only time will tell.

I have hopes for my profession that it will move with this opportunity and grasp what could be an amazing progression. But I also have fears that those who control this same profession, who have a commercial investment in not taking full advantage of this future, will hold us all back for their own advantage and fear of loss.

So now it is up to all of you. I have done my part and I have shone a light on the possible and the potential.

It is now up to the will of people.

I have hope, and so to all my fellow professionals I say, *'May the future be bright and exciting for you all, no matter what that future looks like when it finally arrives'*.

Peter Taylor (aka The Lazy Project Manager).
1 October 2025.

DOI: 10.4324/9781003672357-14

Note

1 Nevil Shute, *In the Wet*, Vintage Classics, 2009.

‘Project managers won’t disappear. But the visible project manager mostly will’.

‘Why did the AI replace the project manager? Because it realised the only risk worth mitigating was the project manager’.

Appendices

About the author

Peter Taylor

Keynote speaker and coach, Peter is the author of the number-one best-selling project management book *The Lazy Project Manager*, along with many other books[1] on Project Management, PMO development, Executive Sponsorship, Transformation Leadership and Speaking Skills.

Peter has built and led some of the largest PMOs in the world with organisations such as Siemens, IBM/Cognos, Kronos/UKG and now Dayforce, where he is the VP Global PMO and Global Customer Office.

He has also delivered over 550 lectures around the world in 28 countries and has been described as 'perhaps the most entertaining and inspiring speaker in the project management world today'.[2]

You can discover more about Peter through his website www.thelazyprojectmanager.com and he is always happy to chat about how he can help you or your organisation through speaking, writing and influencing.

A.1 Other Routledge publications

- *Project Management: It's All Bollocks* (2019).
- *Make Your Business Agile: A Roadmap for Transforming Your Management and Adapting to the 'New Normal'* (2021).
- *AI and the Project Manager: How the Rise of Artificial Intelligence Will Change Your World* (2021).
- *Team Analytics: The Future of High-Performance Teams and Project Success* (2023).
- *Projects: Methods: Outcomes: Methods: Outcomes: The New PMO Model for True Project and Change Success* (2023).
- *The Lazy Winning Project Manager: Embracing Project and Personal Productivity in an AI Empowered World* (2024).

Figure A.1 Peter Taylor – author and speaker

A.2 AI and the Project Manager

AI and the Project Manager by Peter Taylor, published by Routledge, is an accessible yet thought-provoking exploration of how artificial intelligence is reshaping the discipline of project management.

It is a call to action for his profession.

The book begins by demystifying AI, explaining its evolution from early concepts and breakthroughs (like machine learning, natural language processing and expert systems) through to the sophisticated, data-driven tools emerging today. Taylor situates this technological shift in a historical context, tracing how automation has gradually encroached on once-human tasks and highlighting the ways AI can now support or even replace many routine project activities, such as scheduling, reporting, risk prediction and performance tracking.

Rather than portraying AI as a threat, Taylor makes the case that project managers have a tremendous opportunity to elevate their value by embracing these tools. He illustrates how AI can handle up to 80% of administrative and analytical workload, freeing human professionals to focus on leadership, stakeholder engagement and fostering collaborative cultures that no algorithm can replicate at this time.

Figure A.2 AI and the Project Manager book (2021).

The book draws on real-world examples and emerging case studies to show AI-powered assistants spotting early signs of project trouble, recommending interventions and matching the right talent to the right tasks, and being an amazing 'digital partner'.

Taylor balances optimism with caution, emphasising the pitfalls of biased data, lack of transparency and overreliance on automation.

He challenges readers to consider whether traditional certifications and methods will remain relevant in a world where AI can learn and adapt faster than any manual process.

Ultimately, the book is both a guide and a reflection on the future of the profession, as well as a call for project managers to reimagine their role, not as task administrators but as human-centred leaders working in partnership with intelligent machines.

A.3 PMassistant.ai

PMassistant.ai is an AI-powered assistant built to help project managers cut through meeting clutter and keep teams aligned without the manual grunt work.

https://pmassistant.ai/

Instead of digging through notes or chasing down updates, PMassistant .ai turns meeting transcripts into clean, actionable summaries. It captures who attended, what was decided and what needs to happen next.

It's made for fast-moving teams where clarity is critical and time is tight. Whether you're leading a roadmap review, sprint planning or a project implementation, the tool keeps track of everything so project managers can focus on driving outcomes, not managing follow-ups.

Unlike generic AI bots, PMassistant.ai is built with structured prompts rooted in real project management workflows. It's designed to surface the next steps, follow-ups and key details before you even have to think about them.

It's simple to use, focuses on what matters and delivers clear, usable output from the meetings you're already having.

Progress shouldn't get lost in the transcript, because decisions, deadlines and next steps need to be captured clearly and followed through.

A.4 Project Flux

Project Flux represents the leading voice in exploring artificial intelligence's transformative impact on project delivery and management. Founded by James Garner and co-host Yoshi Soornack, Project Flux serves as a critical bridge between the rapidly evolving world of AI technology and the practical realities faced by project professionals across industries.

At its core, Project Flux operates as a comprehensive platform encompassing a podcast, newsletter and blog that collectively address the most pressing questions facing project managers in an AI-driven future. The platform's mission centres on helping project professionals navigate the complex landscape of artificial intelligence adoption, from understanding emerging technologies to implementing practical solutions that enhance project outcomes.

The Project Flux podcast features in-depth conversations with technology leaders, AI innovators and forward-thinking project professionals who are actively shaping the future of work. These discussions go beyond surface-level AI hype to explore real-world applications, implementation challenges and the human implications of technological transformation in project environments.

Through its newsletter and blog content, Project Flux provides regular insights into AI developments specifically relevant to project delivery, offering analysis that bridges the gap between technical innovation and practical application. The platform serves thousands of project professionals worldwide who recognise that understanding AI isn't optional – it's essential for remaining relevant in an increasingly automated world.

Project Flux stands as an essential resource for any project professional serious about understanding and preparing for the AI revolution in project management.

Visit projectflux.ai to join the community or subscribe to the newsletter at https://projectflux.beehiiv.com/subscribe

A.5 Additional reference material

A.5.1 Project manager's uniform

When my youngest son was at junior school, they had a thing called 'bring a parent to school to tell the kids about their job'.

Never got invited!

Sigh.

A policeman got invited and talked about road safety and crime reporting and things like that. Quite popular.

A nurse came in and talked about cuts and bruises and first aid and things like that. Quite popular.

And who else?

Oh yes, a fireman came in and talked about what to do in the event of a fire or if someone was in trouble. Very popular (especially with the Mums apparently).

Now think about this. What do these folks have in common?

They have a uniform! Yes, they have an actual 'look at what I do' uniform. Respect!

Imagine if we had a project management uniform. Cape, bright underpants, capital 'P' on our chest. Wow!

Next day at work as you walked through the office, people would cheer and say, 'thank goodness, it's a project manager, everything will all be OK now'.

Maybe set this as a challenge at your next team meeting – design the project manager's uniform; it could be fun.

A.5.2 A short history of Artificial Intelligence (AI)

Early Ideas

- Ancient myths and automata: Stories of artificial beings (e.g., Greek myth of Talos, and medieval automata).

1940s–1950s Foundations

- Alan Turing (1950): Proposed the Turing Test ('Can machines think?').
- Norbert Wiener: Founded cybernetics (feedback and control systems).

Birth of AI (1956)

- 1956: Term 'Artificial Intelligence' coined at the Dartmouth Conference (John McCarthy, Marvin Minsky, Claude Shannon).
- Early optimism: Belief AI would soon match human intelligence.

Early Programmes (1950s–1960s)

- Logic Theorist (1955): First reasoning programme (Newell and Simon).
- ELIZA (1966): Early chatbot simulating a psychotherapist.
- Shakey the Robot (1969): First robot combining perception and action.

AI Winters (1970s–1980s)

- Funding cuts due to overpromises and limited computing power.
- Slow progress in natural language understanding and knowledge representation.

Revival and Expert Systems (1980s)

- Expert systems: Rule-based programmes solving domain-specific problems (e.g., MYCIN for medical diagnosis).
- Commercial success, but systems brittle and hard to maintain.

Machine Learning Rises (1990s–2000s)

- Shift from rule-based AI to learning from data.
- 1997: IBM's Deep Blue defeats world chess champion Garry Kasparov.
- Growth in data availability and computational power.

Modern AI (2010s–present)

- Deep Learning revolution:
  - 2012: AlexNet wins ImageNet – deep neural networks outperform previous approaches.
  - Breakthroughs in speech recognition, translation, image generation.
- 2016: AlphaGo beats Go champion Lee Sedol.
- Transformer models (2017): Google's 'Attention is All You Need' is the basis for GPT models.
- ChatGPT[3] (2022): Large language models reach mainstream adoption.
- Generative AI (2023–present): Text, image, audio and video generation at scale.

A.5.2.1 Types of AI (Narrow, General and Superintelligence)

Understanding the different types of Artificial Intelligence is essential to grasp both the current capabilities and future potential of AI in project management.

Narrow AI (ANI – Artificial Narrow Intelligence)

Also called Weak AI, this is AI designed to perform a specific task or a narrow set of tasks (often with superhuman speed or accuracy) but without true understanding or general intelligence.

Examples in Project Management:

- Automated scheduling tools.
- Risk prediction algorithms.
- Chatbots that answer PM-related questions.
- Generative tools that create reports or emails.

Nearly all AI in use today, including the tools automating elements of project management, are considered Narrow AI, which excels at defined tasks but cannot adapt beyond its programming.

General AI (AGI – Artificial General Intelligence)

Also called Strong AI, this refers to a still-hypothetical form of AI with human-level cognitive abilities where AGI would understand, learn and apply knowledge across diverse domains, such as reasoning, creativity, problem-solving and emotional intelligence.

Examples in project management:

- A system that could manage any type of project without any prior training.
- An AI that could understand an organisation's culture, politics and goals, then independently adjust its approach accordingly.

AGI does not exist yet, as it remains a research goal at this time, and many experts believe we are decades away from achieving it, and yet progress in the broader AI field is moving at an astonishingly fast speed, so who can really tell.

Superintelligence (ASI – Artificial Superintelligence)

A theoretical AI that surpasses human intelligence in every field, including science, creativity and social intelligence. It would be capable of self-improvement and potentially make decisions beyond human comprehension.

- Hypothetical only and often the domain of speculative fiction or long-term foresight discussions

ASI is not relevant to current project management practice, while naturally being intriguing in its future potential.

Ethical and control discussions often revolve around this conceptual stage of AI development, it should be noted.

A.5.3 Key AI capabilities relevant to project management

Some guidance and examples on thinking about AI capabilities in the project profession.

- Natural Language Processing (meeting summaries and sentiment analysis).
- Machine Learning (predictive risk analysis).
- Computer Vision (where applicable).
- Generative AI (auto-generating status reports, and coordinating communication).
- Autonomous Agents (AI managing workflows and decisions).

A.5.4 Why ethics in AI matters

AI systems can amplify both efficiency and inequality. Decisions made by algorithms have unintended consequences if not properly designed, monitored and understood.

Here are some potential areas to think about:

- **Bias in data and algorithms**
  - AI learns from historical data, which may contain human biases (such as gender, or racial, or role-based disparities), and if not corrected, then the AI may replicate or even exacerbate these biases in project assignments, team composition or performance assessments.
  - *Example: An AI system that consistently assigns leadership roles to team members from certain backgrounds because the training data reflects past trends.*
  - **Action:** Regularly audit datasets and algorithmic outputs for bias and ensure the use of diverse representative data when training models.
- **Transparency and explainability**
  - Project teams need to understand *why* an AI made a certain recommendation.
  - *If the AI's reasoning is just a 'black box' then trust will erode.*
  - **Action:** Use 'explainable AI' (XAI) models where possible, and demand clarity from vendors about how AI decisions are made.
- **Accountability and human oversight**
  - AI can assist with decisions, but final accountability must remain with the human, delegating critical decisions (budget cuts, resource removal, etc.) entirely to AI risks potential legal, ethical and reputational fallout.
  - **Action:** Establish clear roles for both AI and the human element and define escalation paths when any AI outputs seem questionable.

A.5.5 An AI Glossary

- **Privacy and consent**
  - AI systems may need to process sensitive personal or project data, but using this data without consent or safeguards can breach privacy laws.

    - **Action:** Ensure AI systems comply with GDPR or local privacy regulations and be transparent with teams about how their data is used.
- **Security risks**
    - AI systems can be vulnerable to manipulation (the idea of malicious feeding of 'poisoned' data) or breaches that expose confidential project data.
    - **Action:** Integrate AI into your organisation's cybersecurity framework and secure both the models and the data that they rely on.

The invisible project manager may be powered by AI, but ethics must remain visible and intentional since responsible AI isn't just good governance, but it's smart project management.

The Invisible Project Manager is inevitable (I hope that you now agree), but it must not be morally blind, legally ambiguous or socially tone-deaf.

Before we entrust AI with our projects, we must ensure it has not only capability, but accountability.

Because in the end, no matter how intelligent the system becomes, it still operates in our world and must be judged by our standards.

A.5.6 A little bit of laziness (in case you missed it)

An extract from (possibly the bestselling project management book of all time) – *The Lazy Project Manager* (Editions 1 and 2) then *The Lazy Winning Project Manager* (2024) – by Peter Taylor.

Being lazy doesn't equate to being unintelligent. Instead, productive laziness entails achieving success with less effort. When I advocate for 'lazy' project management, I'm not suggesting we do nothing at all. Sitting around idly would be foolish and detrimental to our careers. Lazy, in this context, doesn't imply stupidity.

Rather, I propose a more focused approach to project management. It's about directing our efforts where they truly count, rather than busying ourselves with trivial tasks that others could handle or that don't require attention at all. Welcome to the concept of 'Productive Laziness'.

On the following pages, I delve deeper into what productive laziness means and how you can implement these strategies in your own projects. I'm not inherently lazy, but I recognise the importance of balancing work with other aspects of life. My goal is success, both in my projects and in maintaining a fulfilling personal life.

Lazy doesn't lead to failure. As a Lazy Project Manager, I've learned to strike this balance effectively, ensuring successful outcomes for both my projects and my career, while still leaving time for family and personal pursuits. So, you can stick to the frantic pace of traditional project management, or you can join me in the pursuit of efficient success from the comfort of life's metaphorical comfy chair.

Table A.1 An AI terminology glossary

Term	*Definition*
AI (Artificial Intelligence)	Simulation of human intelligence by machines
AGI (Artificial General Intelligence)	Hypothetical AI that can perform any intellectual task a human can
Algorithm	Step-by-step instructions for solving problems or performing tasks
Annotation	Labelling data to train AI models
Bias	Skewed results in AI due to flawed training data or model assumptions
Big Data	Very large datasets used for analytics and AI training
Black Box	AI system whose internal workings are not easily understood
Chatbot	AI that simulates human conversation
Classification	Assigning data to predefined categories
Computer Vision	AI those processes and interprets visual information
Data Mining	Analysing large datasets to find patterns
Deep Learning	Subset of ML using multi-layered neural networks
Dataset	A structured collection of data
Ethical AI	Ensuring AI systems are fair, transparent and beneficial
Explainable AI (XAI)	AI systems that make their decision-making understandable to humans
Fine-Tuning	Adapting a pre-trained model to a specific task using additional data
Feature Extraction	Identifying key data characteristics useful for model training
Generative AI	AI that creates new content (e.g., text, images)
Ground Truth	Accurate reference data for evaluating models
Hallucination	AI generating false or misleading outputs as if they were factual
Hyperparameters	Settings that define model training behaviour
Inference	Using a trained model to make predictions
Input Data	Data provided to the model for processing
Labelling	Assigning meaningful tags or classes to data
Large Language Model (LLM)	AI trained on massive text datasets to understand and generate language
Learning Rate	Controls how much the model changes during training
Machine Learning (ML)	Enabling systems to learn and improve from data without being explicitly programmed
Model	A trained algorithm that makes predictions based on data
Natural Language Processing (NLP)	AI focused on understanding and generating human language
Neural Network	Algorithm inspired by the human brain used in deep learning
Node	A computational unit in a neural network

(*Continued*)

Table A.1 (Continued)

Term	*Definition*
Overfitting	Model performs well on training data but poorly on new data
Output	Result produced by an AI model
Pre-training	Initial broad training before fine-tuning a model
Prompt Engineering	Crafting inputs to get desired outputs from generative AI
Reinforcement Learning	AI learns via rewards and penalties through interaction with an environment
Retraining	Updating a model with new data
Supervised Learning	ML where data includes labels or correct answers
Synthetic Data	Artificially generated data for training or testing models
Token	A unit of text (word, character, etc.) in NLP models
Training Data	The data used to teach an AI model
Transformer	Deep learning model architecture used in NLP (e.g., GPT, BERT)
Unsupervised Learning	ML where the model learns from unlabelled data
Underfitting	Model is too simple to learn the data patterns
Validation Data	Used to fine-tune and evaluate a model during training
Vectorisation	Turning data (especially text) into numerical format

A.5.6.1 The science behind the laziness

This isn't just a whimsical notion; behind this theory lies a foundation of science, history and even a singing bear.

The Pareto Principle,[4] commonly known as the 80/20 rule, suggests that for many occurrences, 80% of the outcomes stem from 20% of the causes. While this principle finds practical application in numerous scenarios, it's often misused. Merely fitting 80% of cases doesn't automatically qualify a solution as adhering to the 80/20 rule; it's crucial to recognise that such a solution requires only 20% of the resources needed to address all cases.

Originally proposed by management thinker Joseph M. Juran, the principle bears the name of Italian economist Vilfredo Pareto, who noted that 80% of Italy's property was owned by 20% of its population. The underlying assumption is that a small number of causes predominantly drive the results in any given situation.

For instance, '20% of clients may account for 80% of sales volume'. While not absolute, this approximation is often fairly accurate and can inform future decision-making. The Pareto Principle extends beyond business into everyday life: We might find that we wear our favourite 20% of clothes about 80% of the time or spend 80% of our time with just 20%

of our acquaintances. Many companies receive 80% of their revenue from 20% of customers.

It's important to distinguish the Pareto Principle from Pareto efficiency, which was indeed introduced by Vilfredo Pareto himself. His contributions to economics, sociology and moral philosophy, particularly in income distribution and individual choice analysis, are noteworthy. The principle reminds us, project managers, to focus on the vital 20%.

Woody Allen[5] once quipped that '80% of success is showing up', but I've witnessed projects where mere physical presence didn't equate to progress, let alone any success. Instead, it's better to recognise that only 20% of our daily tasks truly matter, yielding 80% of our results. Identifying and prioritising these tasks is the essence of 'Productive Laziness', ensuring efficient outcomes with minimal effort.

A.5.6.2 The intelligence behind the laziness

It's not enough to simply embrace laziness; to truly excel, you must be lazy in a smart way. Productive Laziness isn't just about idleness; it's a powerful blend of laziness and intelligence. Those who master this combination possess a distinct advantage in society, especially in leadership roles within organisations.

This concept isn't new; it has historical roots, notably demonstrated in the Prussian Army by Helmuth Karl Bernhard Graf von Moltke, a revered strategist of the 19th century. Moltke revolutionised military tactics during his tenure as Chief of the Prussian army, implementing modern methods of army direction.

Moltke's approach to categorising his officer corps remains influential today, applicable not only to military leadership but also to project management and other forms of leadership. He divided officers into four distinct types based on their mental and physical attributes.

Type 'A' officers, mentally dull and physically lazy, were assigned straightforward tasks but offered little potential for advancement. Type 'B' officers, bright and energetic, tended to micromanage and lacked leadership qualities. Type 'C' officers, dull but energetic, posed challenges requiring constant supervision and were often dismissed.

However, it was the type 'D' officers – mentally bright yet physically lazy – that Moltke deemed most suitable for high command. These individuals possessed the intelligence to understand what needed to be done but were motivated by their laziness to seek the most efficient solutions. In essence, they epitomised success through minimal effort.

So, which type do you aspire to be? Type 'A', 'B', 'C' or 'D'? It's a challenging choice, indeed.

Smart lazy individuals hold a significant advantage and are ideally suited for leadership positions. *The Lazy Project Manager* embraces these principles, assuming the reader possesses intelligence and aims to refine their lazy skills to ascend to the top right-hand side of Moltke's diagram. By doing so, not only will projects become more successful, but individuals will also be recognised as competent leaders, primed for future roles.

In the words of Walter Chrysler,[6] 'Whenever there is a hard job to be done, I assign it to a lazy man; he is sure to find an easy way of doing it'.

A.5.6.3 *The 'Goldilocks' equation*

There is a word 'lagom' that you most probably have not heard of, unless you are Scandinavian – its meaning kind of summarises this whole productive laziness thing.

'Lagom' is a Swedish term that means 'just the right amount' or 'not too much, not too little'. It can be translated in various ways, such as 'in moderation', 'in balance', 'perfect-simple', 'just enough', 'ideal' and 'suitable' (in terms of quantities). Unlike words like 'sufficient' and 'average', which imply some level of abstinence, scarcity or failure, 'lagom' conveys a sense of appropriateness, though not necessarily perfection. The quintessential Swedish proverb 'Lagom är bäst', literally 'The right amount is best', is also translated as 'Enough is as good as a feast', or 'There is virtue in moderation'.

It can be thought of as the 'Goldilocks'[7] equation where what you have is not too much, not too little, but just right.

Think of Goldilocks when you are considering your own efforts and outputs.

A.5.6.4 *It's a jungle (book) out there*

Doo be doo be doo: Inspiration from a great 'character' actor.

You know that scene from *Jungle Book*, one of Disney's great films,[8] where the bear, Baloo, encourages Mowgli, the boy child, to think about life in a different way?

Baloo sings about looking for just the bare necessities of life, about trying to relax and cool it, and not spending any time looking for things that are worth it or can't even be found. Or put it another way, he is explaining to Mowgli that life using the good old 80/20 rule can be a lot less stressful.

For me 'The Bare Necessities' could well be the 'Productive Lazy' theme tune. Check out the full lyrics some time, take a stroll down memory lane and watch the film one more time and enjoy Baloo the (singing) Bear teach you all about the bare necessities of life that will come to you.

If that isn't good old doo be doo be doo productive laziness I don't know what is!

Notes

1 Many of which he has cunningly managed to reference in this book (shameless promotion never hurts).
2 To be clear, this was not a quote from his mother.
3 ChatGPT has experienced rapid growth since its launch, becoming one of the most popular generative AI applications. Within a short time, it reached 100 million monthly active users and continues to grow, with an estimated 180.5 million monthly active users. The platform's website traffic has also skyrocketed, with billions of visits recorded.
4 The Pareto principle (also known as the 80/20 rule, the law of the vital few and the principle of factor sparsity) states that for many outcomes, roughly 80% of consequences come from 20% of causes (the 'vital few'). In 1941, management consultant Joseph M. Juran developed the concept in the context of quality control and improvement after reading the works of Italian sociologist and economist Vilfredo Pareto, who wrote in 1906 about the 80/20 connection while teaching at the University of Lausanne[3]. In his first work, Cours d'économie politique, Pareto showed that approximately 80% of the land in the Kingdom of Italy was owned by 20% of the population. The Pareto principle is only tangentially related to Pareto efficiency.
5 Heywood Allen is an American filmmaker, actor and comedian whose career spans more than six decades. Allen has received many accolades, including the most nominations for the Academy Award for Best Original Screenplay.
6 Walter Percy Chrysler was an American industrial pioneer in the automotive industry, an American automotive industry executive and the founder and namesake of the American Chrysler Corporation.
7 *Goldilocks and the Three Bears* is a 19th-century English fairy tale with three versions. The original tale features an impudent old woman who intrudes into the forest home of three anthropomorphic bachelor bears while they are away. She eats some of their porridge, sits on one of their chairs and breaks it, and sleeps in one of their beds. When the bears return and find her, she wakes up, jumps out of the window, and is never seen again. The second version replaces the old woman with a young, naive, blonde-haired girl named Goldilocks. The third and most famous version changes the bachelor bears to a family of three. This story has inspired various interpretations and has been adapted into films, operas and other media. *Goldilocks and the Three Bears* remains one of the most popular fairy tales in the English language.
8 *The Jungle Book* is a 1967 animated feature film, released on 18 October 1967. The 19th animated feature in the Disney animated features canon, it was the last to be produced by Walt Disney, who died during its production. It was inspired by the stories about the feral child Mowgli from the book of the same name by Rudyard Kipling. The movie remains one of Disney's most popular, and contained a number of classic songs, including 'The Bare Necessities' and 'I Wanna Be Like You'. Most of the songs are by Richard M. Sherman and Robert B. Sherman.

Index

For Product Safety Concerns and Information please contact our EU
representative GPSR@taylorandfrancis.com
Taylor & Francis Verlag GmbH, Kaufingerstraße 24, 80331 München, Germany

www.ingramcontent.com/pod-product-compliance
Ingram Content Group UK Ltd.
Pitfield, Milton Keynes, MK11 3LW, UK
UKHW022018180926
475701UK00005B/907
* 9 7 8 1 0 4 1 1 3 9 5 1 5 *